The Face of Denmark

The Museum
of National History
at Frederiksborg Castle
1997

Published in 1997
by the Museum of National History
at Frederiksborg Castle, Denmark,
for the exhibition *The Face of Denmark*
held at the Scottish National Portrait Gallery, Edinburgh,
from 19 June to 31 August 1997.

Exhibition organized by
Mette Bligaard and James Holloway.

The Face of Denmark
Editor: Mette Bligaard
Contributors:
Mette Bligaard (MB), Steffen Heiberg (SH),
Hanne Lopdrup (HL) and Tove Thage (TT).
English translation:
Foreword and introductory essay: David Hohnen.
Catalogue: Joan F. Davidson.
Photographers:
Ole Haupt, Jakob Mydtskov, Hans Petersen,
Kit Weiss and Ole Woldbye.
© Det Nationalhistoriske Museum
på Frederiksborg, 1997.
Graphic design:
Ole Zøfting-Larsen.
Lithography:
Hertz Repro A/S, Copenhagen.
Bound by Durlands Eftf. ApS, Greve.
Printed in Denmark
by Center-Tryk A/S, Holbæk.
ISBN 87-87237-69-5

Cover illustrations:
Frederik V (detail) by Carl Gustaf Pilo, 1751.
The Danish writer *Peter Høeg*
(detail) by Henrik Saxgren, 1993.

Contents

Foreword

The exhibition "The Face of Denmark" is the result of collaboration between two national portrait galleries, the Scottish and the Danish. The two institutions were founded at approximately the same time: the Museum of National History at Frederiksborg Castle in 1878 (but with roots going back to 1812), the Scottish National Portrait Gallery in 1882. Both collections arose from a need for national self-assertion and both are the outcome of extraordinary private patronage of the arts. The founder of the Danish museum was a brewer, that of the Scottish gallery the proprietor of a newspaper. Both institutions are housed in unusual buildings, the Danish one in a royal seat dating from the beginning of the seventeenth century and built by Christian IV, brother-in-law of James VI of Scotland, the Scottish in Sir Robert Rowand Anderson's Gothic Revival palace, specially built for the purpose and in itself a unique architectural monument. The two institutions are also related in terms of collection policies. Although the Frederiksborg Museum is not exclusively a portrait gallery – as it also contains important collections of history paintings and all types of decorative art placed in furnished rooms on chronological principles – the portrait gallery is run on the same lines as the Scottish gallery, for it is the museum's aim continuously to acquire, through purchases or commissions, portraits of important Danish men and women.

The majority of the exhibition's one hundred Danish faces are painted portraits. They are supplemented by a few portrait drawings and portrait sculptures. The exhibition also embraces a selection of photographic portraits from the period between 1952 and the present day. Two-thirds of the exhibited portraits are from the Frederiksborg Museum's collections; the remainder have been lent by other museums or by private owners.

The selection has been made with the aim of demonstrating some main trends in the development of Danish portraiture from the founding of the Royal Danish Academy of Fine Arts in 1754 until the present day. It has not been our intention to assemble a pantheon of the nation's most prominent individuals, although most of the persons are worthy of a national portrait gallery. A peasant woman, a few artists' wives and a child have also been included. The artists are predominantly Danish, but there are some examples of foreign artists who have been active in Denmark for varying lengths of time.

"The Face of Denmark" has been arranged by the Museum of National History at Frederiksborg Castle, which in return will show the exhibition "Four Hundred Years of Scottish Portraits" arranged by the Scottish National Portrait Gallery during the period 5 September - 2 November 1997. We should like to thank all our Scottish colleagues for their splendid collaboration, especially Duncan Thomson, Keeper of the Scottish National Portrait Gallery, James Holloway, Deputy to the Keeper and Julie Lawson, Assistant Keeper.

Mette Bligaard
Director of the Museum of National History at Frederiksborg Castle

The Danish Portrait
– from 1750 until the present day
By Mette Bligaard

Until the middle of the eighteenth century, control of the artistic life of
Denmark rested in the hands of the absolute monarch and his closest
circle. In 1754, however, a step of great significance was taken: on the
king's initiative, an academy of art was founded in Copenhagen with
the aim of training artists and, in particular, of promoting artistic
activity. A systematic and well-organized programme for the tuition of
artists was established on the French model: training in the visual arts
was to conform to a fixed set of rules in the same way as any other
trade or craft.

Tuition was entrusted from the beginning to foreign artists,
amongst whom Frenchmen dominated. The sculptor Jacques-
François-Joseph Saly, who had been summoned to Denmark to
execute an equestrian statue of the king, became the Academy's
director for the first seventeen years. Tuition in sculpture was given by
Louis Auguste le Clerc, and in architecture by Nicolas-Henri Jardin.
The professor of painting was the Swedish portraitist Carl Gustaf Pilo,
who since 1747 had been court painter to Frederik V, founder of the
Royal Danish Academy of Fine Arts.

Pilo was the portrait painter of the Rococo *par excellence*. His own
training had been most inadequate, but he had a natural talent and a
knack of staging the monarch and his family so as to make them
appear like dream-like visions from another world. He painted
Frederik V sitting on a rearing horse in a fantasy landscape and, in
another picture, posing in coronation robes in accordance with
Hyacinthe Rigaud's arrangement, but not bombastically like Louis XIV.
The slightly-built Danish monarch floats lightly and elegantly in an
immaterial space. His English-born queen, Louise, her white-
powdered face and hair in tremendous cascades of lace, brocade and
ermine, holds her head high. Pilo's portraits of royalty are colouristic
masterpieces, painted with thick brushstrokes, often with a
dominance of green and cool blue tones, in which the light plays in
the restless folds of the costumes and gleams in the jewels and

decorations. Portrait painting occupied a low place in the hierarchy of genres that had been established by the French Academy of Art in the seventeenth century and taken over by its Danish offshoot, but for the absolute monarch portraits were of vital importance for propaganda purposes – and Pilo was able to deliver the goods.

However, new winds were blowing from France. The portrait painter Louis Tocqué, who stayed for a while in Copenhagen in 1758 on his way home to France from assignments in Russia, is alleged to have remarked about Pilo that he painted like a Turk, which was not meant as a compliment. The French painter, who was brilliant at achieving strikingly exact likenesses and indicating the psychological characteristics of his sitters, was praised by his contemporaries for his veracity. Although Tocqué spent only six months in Denmark, he managed to execute a number of portraits, and continued to Paris after having received a commission to paint full-length portraits of the Danish royal couple. They were intended for the recently completed mansion (now Christian VII's Mansion at Amalienborg) of the influential Lord Chamberlain and connoisseur Adam Gottlob Moltke, where they were to replace two portraits already supplied by Pilo. The transfer took place in 1762 and was material proof of the fact that Pilo's fate – and thus also that of the Rococo portrait – was sealed.

Contemporary examples of foreign portraiture in the grand style could be studied in the potentate's chamber arranged in the royal palace, Christiansborg, from the end of the 1760s. The leading court painters of Europe each supplied a *portrait d'apparat* for this display room, thirteen in all. From France came Louis-Michel van Loo's portrait of Louis XV, from England Allan Ramsay's of George III and from Spain Anton Raphael Mengs's of Carlos III.

Together with the Italian Pompeo Batoni, the German painter Mengs in particular was to exercise important influence on the Danish artists who had been awarded scholarships by the Royal Academy of Fine Arts and then made their way to Rome to complete their training. The painter Peder Als is a typical representative of this transitional period. He had studied under Pilo, but his art underwent a meta-morphosis during his four-year stay in Rome in 1756–61. A period in Paris, 1761–62, alienated him even further from the Rococo style he had learned in Copenhagen. In Rome, under the influence of Mengs, with whom he became personally acquainted, he adopted a heroic style of portraiture characterized by a calmness and simplicity of composition and a sculptural volume in representation of the human figure. His two portraits of the sculptor Johannes Wiedewelt are of great significance in Danish portraiture. The profile portrait of Wiedewelt (cat. no. 5) is no less than a manifesto. Both the portrait-painter and the sculptor portrayed had been converted to Neo-classicism in Rome, as is demonstrated by the subject's classical posture in profile. He is depicted working on a relief surrounded by Roman ruins, the models on which he based his art.

In 1767, Peder Als was appointed professor of painting, and during the following years Danish-born artists who had been trained at the Academy began to play a more important role. Reforms introduced by the German physician-in-ordinary to the mad king Christian VII, Johann Friedrich Struensee, after being made *Gehejmekabinets-minister* (Minister of the Privy Council) in 1771, resulted in a mood of antipathy throughout the country's administration, including the Royal Academy. Between 1770 and 1774 the French professors Jardin and Saly both left Denmark, and in 1771 Pilo also retired to his home country, Sweden. A law covering nationalization, promulgated in 1776, favoured citizens born within the borders of the Danish realm, that is to say Denmark, Norway and the duchies of Schleswig and Holstein, whenever posts in the civil service were to be filled.

Fortunately, several Danish artists were now ready to take over. Apart from Peder Als, the first generation of Danish-trained portrait painters included Jens Juel, Vigilius Erichsen and the miniaturist Cornelius Høyer, which was too many for the Danish market. There was virtually an export of Danish portrait painters during these years. Vigilius Erichsen went to Russia, where he worked for fifteen years as court painter to Catherine II, and Cornelius Høyer, who in addition to having studied at the Royal Academy had also learned his metier from the French miniaturist Jean-Baptiste Massé, travelled round from one European court to another. But a clientele was also to be found outside the royal courts. During a period in Geneva, 1777–79, Jens Juel painted the Swiss bourgeoisie, including philosophers and scientists – even Goethe sat for him for a drawing whose location is unfortunately no longer known.

Jens Juel became the most widely employed portrait painter of his time. During the years he spent studying abroad, from 1772 to 1780, also visiting Dresden, Rome and Paris, he was influenced by Batoni's and Liotard's portraiture, and perhaps he also saw works by Zoffany and Gainsborough, though he never set foot in England. Juel's concept of his sitter is straightforward and unaffected. He is friendly without either embellishing or idealizing. Anatomy was not his strong point, but he was a master at making flesh tints glow and conveying the texture of fabrics. In Geneva he drew nature into his portraits, but it was not only Alpinists and scientists who wished to be portrayed in

the open air, for even Swiss ladies were painted in natural surroundings, and Juel was an excellent landscapist. His portrait of the
merchant Joseph Greenway (cat. no. 12), which was painted in a
Danish landscape, indicates that Juel was acquainted with contemporary English portraiture. In his group portraits he depicted informal
relationships between parents and children, both in royal families and
his own. He was unafraid to represent his sitters in 'natural' situations.
In one case a noblewoman has bared her breast in readiness to suckle
her child, and in another a prosperous merchant is shown with his
little son crawling on his lap. Juel did this sort of thing sensitively, but
never sentimentally.

Juel died in 1802 after having been a professor at the Royal Academy
for eighteen years while at the same time running a 'portrait factory'
where he employed many assistants. The demand for portraits was
steadily increasing.

The first decade of the nineteenth century was a fateful period for
Denmark. The country had to abandon its hitherto observed
neutrality and was forced to enter into an alliance with France, which
proved to be a great misfortune. In 1801 the English defeated the
Danish fleet at the Battle of Copenhagen and six years later an English
fleet returned and bombarded the city. Denmark had to surrender and
hand over its entire fleet. In 1813 the country went bankrupt, and at
the Congress of Vienna the dissolution of the twin monarchy of
Denmark and Norway was confirmed – Denmark had to cede Norway
to Sweden.

First-rate portrait-painters were scarce during the period after Jens
Juel's death. On the other hand Denmark produced a sculptor in a
class of his own. In 1795, an Icelandic wood-carver's son, born in 1768
or 1770 in Copenhagen, was awarded the Royal Academy's travelling
scholarship, and in 1797 he arrived in Rome, where he lived for the
next 41 years, unaffected by the misfortunes being sustained by his
home country. His name was Bertel Thorvaldsen. Before leaving
Copenhagen he had modelled a portrait bust of the prime minister,
A.P. Bernstorff, fully dressed. The costume and hair are rendered in
detail and the elderly statesman's physiognomy is also finely depicted.
In Rome, Thorvaldsen developed his approach to portraiture by
simplifying all irrelevant facial details yet without sacrificing likeness
and in this way developed a strict portrait style in the Classical
manner. His tremendous production of portrait busts, portrait statues
and several equestrian monuments of both living and historical
persons cemented his reputation. After Antonio Canova's death in
1822 Thorvaldsen was incontestably the greatest sculptor in Italy and
consequently a figurehead in his own country. Several Danish

sculptors worked in his studio in Rome, and Danish portrait sculpture was marked by his influence for several succeeding generations.

In 1814 the Royal Academy in Copenhagen received a sensational demonstration of a young artist's ability as a portrait painter. Christoffer Wilhelm Eckersberg, who had travelled through Europe to complete his studies as a history painter, had painted a portrait of his countryman, Thorvaldsen, in Rome. As had been the case with Peder Als's portrait of Johannes Wiedewelt half a century earlier, this portrait of an artist was not only a manifestation of the portraitist's ability but also of the status of the sitter. Thorvaldsen is represented wearing the black robe of the Academy of San Luca in Rome, and two decorations adorn his breast. The figure is strangely bodiless in the clear light, but all textures are masterfully conveyed. It was portraits of this type that contributed to establish the myth of the visionary artist. The Thorvaldsen portrait caused a stir in Copenhagen, where it was interpreted as being executed in a mannerized French style hitherto unseen in northern latitudes, where French art was no longer very popular. Eckersberg had studied under Jacques-Louis David in Paris (1811–12) where he had adopted the French painter's strict style. In Rome, Ingres lived and worked virtually next door to Eckersberg while the latter was painting his portrait of Thorvaldsen, but it is not known whether the two artists came into contact. At all events, Eckersberg had been strongly influenced by French portraiture. He never tired of claiming that nature and the old masters were his models, but despite his 'realistic' representation of reality there was an element of abstraction in his later portraits. This applies, for example, to his double portrait of the Nathanson sisters from 1820 (fig. 1). The picture of the two young women is composed as relief, two parallel planes being displaced in relation to one another: foremost, the seated woman in profile, captured in a frozen movement; behind her the standing woman, seen *en face*, full length. As always in Eckersberg's portraits the colours are bright and luminously clear and forms are depicted with smoothness and a wealth of detail.

Two years earlier, in 1818, Eckersberg had painted the entire Nathanson family: the Copenhagen merchant, his wife and eight children in their drawing-room, in a similarly strict, relief-like composition. It is a Danish counterpart to the English conversation piece, a genre which in the first half of the nineteenth century was to

Fig. 1. C.W. Eckersberg: *Bella and Hanna Nathanson*. 1820.
The Royal Museum of Fine Arts, Copenhagen

appeal greatly to the Danish bourgeoisie, who at this time were buying portraits on a large scale. It was not a question of group portraits, arranged for representation, but of pictures of defined or anonymous people in luminous rooms engaged in various activities. The painter Jørgen Roed declared that such a picture was "a painting that represents nothing". Emilius Bærentzen was a specialist in these representations, one of which, "The Winter Family" (cat. no. 25), is in the National Gallery of Scotland.

The period from the state bankruptcy until the middle of the nineteenth century has been called – by a posterity with a penchant for labels – the 'golden age' of Denmark's art and intellectual life, and Eckersberg has been designated as the father of Danish painting. In 1818 he had been made a professor at the Royal Academy, a post which he held until his death in 1853. His teaching influenced a long series of artists who devoted themselves to all genres, including portrait painting. But the generation after Eckersberg avoided Paris. They regarded Rome as incontestably the capital of art, and the way to it was through Germany, whose academies, especially the one in Munich, were now frequented by several Danish artists. Contact between Danish and German artists in Rome was moreover lively, and Danish art took on a touch of Biedermeier, particularly in genre paintings of quiet Copenhagen living-rooms.

Among Eckersberg's pupils, one who excelled himself, also as a portraitist, was Christen Købke. As a rule he painted small pictures intended to be hung in the drawing-rooms of the bourgeoisie, and his sitters included fellow artists and members of his family. But occasionally he was commissioned to paint an official portrait, and that of Jens Andreas Graah (a Danish *amtmand,* or chief administrative officer of a county) shows that he fully mastered such assignments.

Strangely enough, the portraitists whom we regard today as being the most gifted were not recognized in leading circles in their own time. Købke was never made a member of the Royal Academy, and C.A. Jensen and Johan Vilhelm Gertner both had to suffer the humiliation, time and again, of being severely condemned by the art critics, despite which they experienced no shortage of commissions. C.A. Jensen painted several portraits for the Royal Portrait Collection, which had been housed in Frederiksborg Castle since 1812. His portraits have a sophisticated simplicity. He gives a penetrating and lively characterization of his sitter, devoid of idealization. As a rule his palette is restricted to a few colours. The black cloth of a man's costume is enlivened by a striking colour accentuation in a decoration, and the jacket of a uniform by the highlights of buttons or epaulettes. C.A. Jensen was also in demand abroad, and for a time worked in both Russia and England. In 1837 he exhibited three portraits at the Royal Academy in London, including one of the Danish archaeologist P.O. Brøndsted, who had excavated the temple at Bassai in the Peleponnese together with the English architect Charles Robert Cockerell. Jensen's portrait of Cockerell, painted in London in 1838, is a minor masterpiece. Cockerell's estimation of the Danish artist was that "he has an accurate talent, naive and keen; but he is hardly enough charlatan in his act or in character to have the success he deserves". In Denmark, where Eckersbergian smoothness was still the ideal, C.A. Jensen was criticized for his brisk style of painting. It was held that his forms were inadequately modelled and that he neglected his sitter's hair, with the result that his pictures appeared unfinished. Traces of brushwork were regarded as new-fangled European flashiness, unacceptable at a time when nationalism was all-important. C.A. Jensen's way of painting was simply stamped as unpatriotic.

Johan Vilhelm Gertner's portrait drawings were brilliant, and in his painted portraits he strove for an almost photographic realism that seemed strange to his contemporaries. One critic wrote: "These portraits are modelled, one feels the flesh." Photography no doubt inspired him in his later years with regard to both composition and a precise representation of reality. In his portraits of royalty, Gertner combines realism with strict formality, and his monarchs have a dignity unseen since the Baroque. He painted the pot-bellied Christian VIII in a revealing profile against a completely black back-ground, and represented Frederik VII as an admiral on the deck of a ship with the accurately registered rigging as an almost abstract back-ground pattern.

The Danish royal house had no Winterhalter, and the life-style at court was not geared to major ceremonial representations. Absolute monarchy had been abolished peacefully in 1848, and the king is notably absent from the large group portrait of the opening session of the Constituent National Assembly in 1848, executed by Constantin Hansen about ten years after the event had taken place. The artist meticulously incorporated all the individual portraits in a previously composed perspective construction of the room. Each individual portrait was created on the basis of a study of the subject, and all are recognizable.

The portrait painters of the following generation mastered the group portrait in a more lavish style. The star performers were P. S. Krøyer and Laurits Tuxen, both of whom had studied open-air painting in the 1870s in Paris. Contact with Paris was now resumed. In Léon Bonnat's studio Danish painters learned a completely new way of treating colour, and their works acquired luminosity and radiance. At the same time they studied old masters such as Velázquez and van Dyck. Portraits became larger. The full-length portrait regained its popularity and was no longer reserved for royalty and the upper classes. In 1878 the Frederiksborg Museum was founded as a museum of national history as well as a national portrait gallery, a successor to the Royal Portrait Gallery, which had previously been housed in Frederiksborg Castle. Portraits in the grand style were required here, whether heroic representations of war heroes, or of prime ministers, scientists and cultural personalities. In addition to Krøyer and Tuxen, artists such as August Jerndorff and Otto Bache were capable of supplying official, ceremonial portraits for the national collection. Krøyer excelled in large group portraits of gatherings of financiers, physicians, engineers and scientists. He painted the soirées of the captains of industry as well as his own artist friends at a seaside resort on a summer's evening, and in every case the light was the unifying element in his pictures, whether provided by the sun, the moon or the new electricity.

Laurits Tuxen developed and perfected the genre: the large-scale group portrait featuring numerous recognizable individuals. He became a much sought-after chronicler of the coronations, weddings, jubilees and other gatherings celebrated by Europe's royal houses. In 1883 he painted a huge group portrait of the entire Danish royal family, and in 1887 he executed a similar painting of Queen Victoria surrounded by her family at Windsor Castle. It was also at Windsor, in 1894, that he painted his swiftly executed study of the seated Queen Victoria, one of the most incredible likenesses of the queen ever to be painted (fig. 2).

Links with French art were extended during the last decades of the nineteenth century. In 1888 the founder of the Ny Carlsberg Glyptotek in Copenhagen, the brewery-owner Carl Jacobsen, arranged a large exhibition of French art in Copenhagen at which Manet and several Impressionists were represented. Paul Gauguin was known in Denmark at an early stage as he had married a Dane and for a while was forced by dire necessity to live in Copenhagen. During a stay in Brittany in 1890 the Danish artist J.F. Willumsen became acquainted with Gauguin and the circle of Symbolists living there, and he was absorbed by the Symbolists' programme and the scientific study of colour. For the Symbolist artist it was not a question of reproducing

Fig. 2. Laurits Tuxen: *Queen Victoria.* 1894.
The Hirschsprung Collection, Copenhagen

reality but of transforming shapes and colours in nature according to the demands of one's mood. The Symbolist portrait painter naturally had to continue taking his point of departure in the individual he had before him, but he simplified and stylized what he saw. Details were eliminated. The Symbolist portrait is characterized by decorative treatment of the surface and emphasizing movement by means of contours. To this was added the interest in colour experiments and working on complementary colours in juxtaposition. In the Symbolist portrait the sitter is often represented in an undefined space against an infinite sky or a closed, flat, gold ground.

Throughout his life, Willumsen continued to cultivate the colouring he had learned in France during the 1890s, also in the few portrait commissions he was given – the intensity of their colours are unparalleled in Danish art (cat. no. 62). However, Symbolism could also assume a different, more restrained form. Einar Nielsen depicted the human condition in austere, stylized portraits. Although he always used specific models for his portraits he often gave them general titles such as *Blind Man, Invalid, Pregnant Woman* or simply *Portrait of a Woman*, as in the case of the portrait of the artist's wife from 1901. In his treatment of colour Nielsen is related to his contemporary Vilhelm Hammershøi, who also preferred to paint figures in rooms using a limited scale of grey tones. Hammershøi's portraits recall those of James McNeill Whistler. Like those of the American painter, they are often merely "arrangements in black and grey". The group portrait of Hammershøi's artist friends, *Five Portraits,* from 1901, is a mysterious modern version of the Last Supper in which five isolated figures are placed round a table in a masterfully conceived composition (fig. 3).

Krøyer's and Tuxen's line was continued, uninfluenced by Symbolism, by painters such as Julius Paulsen and Herman Vedel, who cultivated the naturalistic portrait style until far into the twentieth century. Using an Impressionistic painting style, they worked in the manner of the old masters on the study of colour in an interplay with values. Particularly in Julius Paulsen's one senses Rembrandt's influence.

During the years just before the First World War the decisive impulses came once more from Paris, namely from Cubism in general and Picasso's art in particular. The avant-garde were willing to paint people but displayed little interest in the conventional portrait. They painted themselves, each other, their friends and families, but their aim was neither personal characterization nor the individual. Their portraits are not portraits in the normal sense. They used the human

Fig. 3. Vilhelm Hammershøi: *Five Portraits*. 1901-02. Thielska Galleriet, Stockholm

figure as an excuse for working with purely visual ideas. For them, as the painter Harald Giersing expressed it, surface, colour, line and space were the materials and real content of the art of painting.

At the same time, portrait sculpture enjoyed a revival, the first since Thorvaldsen. Among the sculptors of the generation, Kai Nielsen, Adam Fischer and Johannes Bjerg stand out among the rest. In the Ny Carlsberg Glyptotek, which had been opened as a museum in its own building in 1897, the young sculptors studied recent French sculpture and later also archaic Greek art, but it was in Paris that they received their decisive impulses during the years before the First World War. In particular the works of Auguste Rodin inspired them to a new monumentality. In Kai Nielsen's portraits the sculpture was conceived as a block, regardless of whether the material was black, polished granite, porous limestone or white marble. Nielsen produced a series of outstanding portrait busts during the years before his early death in 1924 and was unafraid to accept a commission for a larger-than-life portrait statue of the canned food manufacturer Mads Rasmussen from 1912-14, which was created for a Neo-classicist domed hall in the manufacturer's own museum. The imposing man stands here in modern dress, his features simplified and stylized: a tremendous granite colossus, portrayed by Nielsen with both dignity and humour.

Adam Fischer, who in Paris had experimented with abstract forms and received impulses from primitive sculpture, returned in the 1920s to the roundness of Classical Greek sculpture. His portrait herm in limestone of his friend the Mexican artist Diego Rivera, from 1918, is a masterpiece of modern Danish sculpture.

For Johannes Bjerg, acquaintanceship with Aristide Maillol in Paris was of decisive importance. Like the French artist, he became absorbed in Greek art. In Bjerg's sculptures the form springs from the qualities of the material as in the grey-black granite bust of the architect P. V. Jensen-Klint, whose costume and facial features are greatly simplified while the distinctive beard and hair are stylized and decorated with rough, wavy lines carved in the black-polished granite (cat. no. 61).

In the inter-war period and right up to the end of the 1970s the portrait was a neglected genre. It was not within the area of figurative painting that conquests were made. Cubism and Surrealism gave rise to a few masterly portraits, but no sitter for an official portrait dared submit to the treatment of these artists, who were scarcely interested in closely defined portrait commissions. Henry Heerup, who went his own way, could treat a physiognomy imaginatively, as when he simplified the characteristic facial features of a well-known revue actress by turning them into arabesques surrounding expanses of bright colour. The result became a kind of signal, a humorous pictogram portrait (cat. no. 64).

Inspired by American pop art and the Super-realism of the 1960s, a Neo-realistic type of portraiture arose during the 1970s that assumed different forms in the hands of artists such as Niels Strøbek, Jørgen Boberg and, much later, Thomas Kluge. They all use a super-realistic technique that in Strøbek's case is employed to account for everything seen: the model, the room, the various details in the space surrounding the model, are all of equal importance. The portraits possess an unassuming naiveté and 'honesty', which in Strøbek's latest works has been replaced by a certain monumentality. Boberg uses his masterful technical ability to imbue his sitters with a metaphysical, surrealistic tinge, isolating them in barren spaces or moonlit landscapes bathed in a bluish-green light. The young painter Thomas Kluge makes use of another form of realism. His portrait subjects are also isolated in dark, neutral spaces in which the figure appears in cold light from the side. Unaffected truthfulness does not exist. Kluge balances on the razor edge between honesty and exposure, as for example in the little portrait of Queen Margrethe from 1996 (cat. no. 81).

In other artists, working with colour forms the point of departure for their portraiture, as in the case of Kurt Trampedach, whose roots are in the Neo-realism of the 1970s. In Trampedach's portraits the temperament of the artist seems to be transferred to the sitter, as in the strict, almost diabolical portrait of a Danish bishop (cat. no. 71), reputedly a mild man. Trampedach is a bold colourist who pastes paint thickly on to his canvas and then scrapes and scratches it. An important colourist of another type is Preben Hornung. With his keen sense of observation he has been able to grasp the particular stature of a figure and then place it in the picture surface with the same sense of pictorial composition as he had used to create his non-figurative pictures earlier in his career. It is not that he disregards portrait likeness, but sometimes he chooses to depersonify his portraits, for example in his three portraits of Denmark's present queen. Here it is not through physiognomy but posture and clothing that the sitter's identity as a monarch is revealed. Hornung's portraits of Margrethe II are queen icons.

Peter Martensen is generally concerned in his art with the anonymous person as passive spectator amongst other anonymous persons. Like many of the artists of our time, particularly the German Gerhard Richter, with whom he has certain points in common, Martensen employs photography and the TV-image as an intermediary in his artistic creativity. His powerful, almost monochrome portrait of the aging politician Poul Hartling from 1996 (cat. no. 77) came into being face to face with the 83-year-old sitter, not as a momentary impression but rather as a concentrate of memories of a person observed over a long period of time.

Work is in progress on a great many forms of expression in the portrait art of our time. Nobody can remain unaffected by photography and the endless flow of digitalized pictures spewed at us by modern media. The borderlines between art forms are becoming blurred. Unrestrained by academic conventions, artists are now crossing the borders of the narrow genre categories of former times. The concept of portraiture is being expanded. The unpopular, officially commissioned portrait – the trade mark of national portrait galleries – can be reinterpreted in our age and take on many astonishing forms, but the human being will still remain the point of departure.

Cultivation of the art of portraiture is an international metier. As will have emerged from the above, Denmark's art of portraiture has developed over the centuries in a continual interplay with major European trends. Whether the one hundred faces of Denmark selected for this exhibition make it justifiable to speak of a special Danish art of portraiture must be left to the non-Danish spectator to decide.

Catalogue

1 Carl Gustaf Pilo 1711–1793
Frederik V 1723–1766

Frederik V was not an outstanding king, but he knew how to choose competent advisers. In cultural respects, Denmark reached a zenith during his reign. 1754 saw the founding of the Royal Academy of Fine Arts, the purpose of which was to train a sufficient number of architects and artists to meet the needs of the court and the nation. Several prominent foreign artists were attached to the Academy, including the French sculptor Jacques-François-Joseph Saly, his countryman, the architect Nicolas-Henri Jardin, and the Swedish painter Carl Gustaf Pilo. These artists gave art in Denmark a cosmopolitan character. At the same time, tuition at the Academy raised the level of domestic artists and in the process paved the way for Denmark's so-called 'golden age'.

Carl Gustaf Pilo came to Denmark in 1741, became Court painter in 1747 and that same year painted the official coronation picture of the king and queen. For the next twenty-five years he was the preferred painter of the court and the aristocracy. In 1772 political conditions forced him to leave Denmark and return to Sweden.

The portrait of Frederik V, painted in 1751, demonstrates his ability to combine the traditional, rather military style of the official portrait with the lightness and elegance of the Rococo.

S.H.

1751
Oil on canvas
Inscribed on the
back: peint par
Pilo 1751
148.5 x 114 cm
Frederiksborg
Museum

Frederik V, King of Denmark and Norway, reigned 1746–1766

2 | Vigilius Erichsen 1722–1782
Queen Juliane Marie 1729–1796

Vigilius Erichsen was the last great Danish representative of official state portraiture. Even within this inherently conservative genre he was distinctively traditionalist. The compositions were painstaking, the colouring was clear and fresh, elegant but lacking the airiness of Pilo. Lack of recognition drove Erichsen to try his fortune abroad, and he made a career for himself as court painter to Empress Catherine II in St Petersburg, where he painted a number of monumental portraits of the Empress. After 15 years in Russia he returned to Denmark in 1772 and was attached to the Danish court. Catherine II also continued to make use of his talents. For the Empress's portrait gallery he painted a large full-length picture of the widowed Queen Juliane Marie, in 1776. The picture exhibited here is a repeated version in smaller format painted two years later. The Queen is pointing at a portrait bust of her deceased husband, Frederik V.

S.H.

1778
Oil on canvas
72.5 x 55 cm
Inscribed:
V. Erichsen. Pinx.
1778
The Royal Museum
of Fine Arts,
Copenhagen

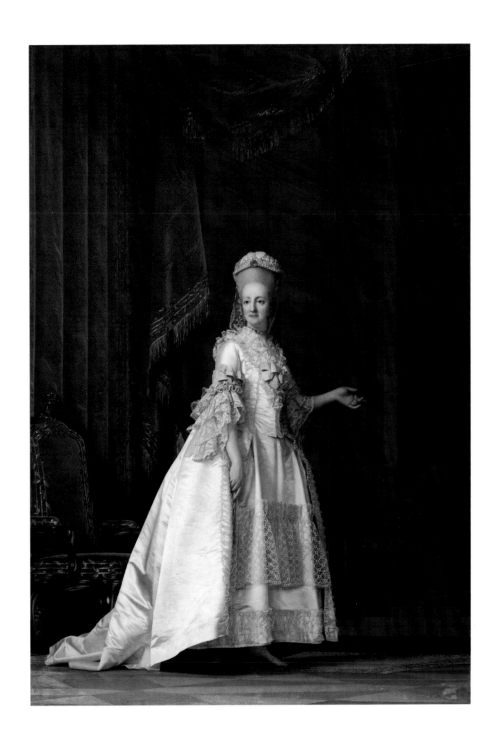

Juliane Marie of Braunschweig-Wolfenbüttel, Queen of Denmark

3 | Vigilius Erichsen 1722–1782
Lorenz Spengler 1720–1807

Among the few paintings by Vigilius Erichsen known from the period before he travelled to Russia are the two portraits of Lorenz Spengler and his wife. Spengler was an immigrant from Switzerland. He was employed as an artist craftsman at the court and made quantities of objects of amber, tortoiseshell and ivory. He made artificial teeth of ivory and narwhal tusk. In addition he was a major collector, e.g. of mechanical objects, shells and other *naturalia*. In 1771 he became Keeper of the Royal Cabinet of Curiosities, an office for which, with his combination of antiquarian and scientific interests, he was well-suited. He viewed the collections of the Cabinet of Curiosities as an entity and fought against all attempts to split them into special collections. He is portrayed holding one of his ivory works in his hand.

S.H.

Oil on canvas
78.5 x 62 cm
The Royal Museum
of Fine Arts,
Copenhagen

4 | Vigilius Erichsen 1722–1782
Gertrud Sabina Trott 1739–1789

The rose which the tender-aged Gertrud Sabine Trott is holding in front of her chest indicates that the picture was painted on the occasion of her marriage to Lorenz Spengler in 1756. The painting is a counterpart to that of Spengler, but is lighter and more refined in its range of colours.

S.H.

Oil on canvas
78 x 62 cm
The Royal Museum
of Fine Arts,
Copenhagen

Lorenz Spengler, ivory-turner and Keeper of the Royal Cabinet of Curiosities

Gertrud Sabina Trott, wife of Lorenz Spengler

5 | Peder Als 1726–1776
Johannes Wiedewelt 1731–1802

In 1754, when Peder Als was accepted as a student in the newly-established Academy of Fine Arts in Copenhagen, he had already about a decade earlier worked as a pupil of the portrait-painter Carl Gustaf Pilo. In 1755 Als won the major gold medal and travelled on the Academy's first scholarship to Rome, where he stayed until 1761; from there he went to Paris for a year. After his return to Copenhagen he became a member of the Academy, as a portrait-painter, in 1764, and became professor in 1766. In that year he submitted this profile-portrait of his friend Johannes Wiedewelt, the sculptor, painted in Rome. With this heroic artist-portrait, Neo-classicism made its entry into Danish portrait-painting.

Wiedewelt, like Peder Als, was converted to Neo-classicism in Rome, where he became acquainted with Anton Raphael Mengs and Pompeo Batoni, and was a close associate of the German archaeologist Johann Joachim Winckelmann, who came to have great significance for him. Wiedewelt is depicted in the portrait in the process of carving a classical relief; after his return to Denmark in 1763 he made the sepulchral monuments for Christian VI and Frederik V for the Danish royal burial place in Roskilde Cathedral. His 54 abstract-allegorical monuments to Danish heroes and heroines, dating from 1777–89 and displayed in the memorial park at Jægerspris Palace, are among the most unusual sculptural achievements of the time.

M.B.

1766
Oil on canvas
82 x 65.8 cm
The Royal Danish
Academy of Fine
Arts

Johannes Wiedewelt, sculptor

6 | Peder Als 1726–1776
Queen Caroline Mathilde 1751–1775

In 1766 the 15-year-old English Princess Caroline Matilda, daughter of
Frederick, Prince of Wales and sister of George III, was married to her
cousin, the 18-year-old Danish king Christian VII. Five years later she
was divorced from her husband, separated from her children and sent
into exile in Celle in Hannover, where she died at the age of 24. She
had been found guilty of adultery, and her lover was executed.
The English painter Francis Cotes had painted several charming
portraits of the young princess. The portraits executed of her in
Denmark differed considerably and clearly reflect the watershed that
Danish portraiture had reached during these years. Carl Gustaf Pilo
painted her as an ethereal Rococo beauty and Jens Juel as a solidly-
built woman, but Peder Als, who in 1766 had been appointed 'History
and Portrait Painter to the Royal Danish Court' depicted her – to the
astonishment of his contemporaries – in provocative male attire. The
profile portrait drawn by Als, which shows the queen's chubby features
and full lips, is typical of his Neo-classical style. It is simple, dignified
and quite devoid of flattery. In 1771 Als was asked to paint another
portrait of the queen. It was commissioned by Johann Friedrich
Struensee, the queen's lover, who requested a representation in the
style familier moderne, in other words an intimate picture of the
queen as mother. Als made several sketches for this painting, but as
a consequence of the queen's being disowned they were never
completed.

M.B.

Probably 1771
Pastel
62 x 50 cm
Inscribed: P. Als ad
viv. delineav.
Frederiksborg
Museum

Caroline Mathilde, Queen of Denmark and Norway

7

Georg Mathias Fuchs 1719–1797
Johan Michael Iselin 1754–1756

1765
Oil on canvas
118 x 82 cm
Frederiksborg
Museum

In 1753 G.M. Fuchs arrived in Denmark, and was given work on the interior decoration of Fredensborg Palace. As a young man he had been an apprentice for six years with Jacopo Amigoni in Venice. In 1754 he became a student at the newly-established Royal Academy of Fine Arts in Copenhagen.

In 1765 Fuchs was given an unusual portrait commission. A wealthy merchant, Reinhard Iselin, who had built up a flourishing trading house, desired to have a portrait painted of his first-born son, Johan Michael Iselin, who had died in 1756 at the age of two.

In spite of the sad circumstances Fuchs has managed to produce a charming version of a child with fine details such as the brilliantly painted straw hat with flowers. In Fuchs's work it is interesting to see the light, fine balancing of colours with the delicate pinks and bluish nuances, which he brought back from Venice.

The little boy is wearing a rose-coloured jacket, white embroidered waistcoat and matching stockings. The white pleated trousers diverge in their fullness from the usual Rococo style close-fitting knee-breeches. The appearance is of a healthy blue-eyed child with a clear skin. Only the black stock indicates sorrow, i.e. the parents's grief for the lost child. The depiction of the child out-of-doors, with a dog and a bird, reflect some influence from Rousseau's theories on education, which became fashionable after the publication of *Emile* in 1762. It is obvious that the artist did not have his subject in front of him. The proportions are awkward. The legs are short, like those of a two-year-old, but the face would fit with a rather older child. The painter may possibly have been familiar with Hogarth's *The Graham Children*, which in fact depicts several children in an indoor scene, but the figure of the seated boy who is absorbed with a bird in a cage looks almost as if it has been copied from it.

H.L.

Johan Michael Iselin

8 | Jens Juel 1745–1802
Jacques-François-Joseph Saly 1717–1776

The French sculptor Jacques-François-Joseph Saly was summoned to
Denmark in 1753 to execute an equestrian statue of Frederik V. The
statue was finally erected in 1771 in the octagonal Amalienborg
Square, which formed the centre of a new quarter, Frederiksstaden
(Frederik's Town) in Copenhagen. This prestigious urban project was
launched to mark the 300th anniversary of the commencement of the
Oldenborg dynasty.

Saly was the director of the new Royal Danish Academy of Fine Arts
for its first seventeen years and did not leave Denmark until 1774.
During his long stay in the country he executed a number of excellent
portrait busts of the king, members of the court and his artist
colleagues.

The young Jens Juel painted Saly's portrait just before setting out on
a long study tour through Germany, Italy, France and Switzerland.
He had still not seen the great portraiture of Europe, but was already
obviously acquainted with the French portrait convention of the
period. The elegantly dressed, gesticulating Frenchman is seen in
front of a statuette of his own major work, Frederik V's equestrian
monument. The characterization is sympathetic and perhaps a little
superficial, but Juel's skill in reproducing fabrics is already clearly in
evidence.

M.B.

1772
Oil on canvas
82 x 67 cm
Signed:
J. Juel pinx 1772
The Royal Museum
of Fine Arts,
Copenhagen

Jacques-François-Joseph Saly, sculptor

9 | Jens Juel 1745–1802
Johan Frederik Clemens 1748–1831

This portrait of the engraver Johan Frederik Clemens was painted by
his close friend, Jens Juel, in Paris in 1776; the two Danish artists
stayed there for a period in the mid-1770s in the course of extensive
travels supported by the Royal Academy of Fine Arts in Copenhagen.
Clemens was the most significant engraver of his generation, and his
works included a large number of engravings made from Jens Juel's
portraits. In the spring of 1792 he visited London, where he was given
the task of making an engraving from the painting *The Death of
General Montgomery in the Attack on Quebec* (1775) by the American
artist John Trumbull, and where he also received commissions to
make engravings from several other paintings by Trumbull and by
Benjamin West. Among the major works by Clemens are the large
engraving of *The Battle of Copenhagen, 2 April 1801*, from C. A.
Lorenzen's painting in Frederiksborg Museum.

   Jens Juel depicts his artist friend sitting with a copper sheet in front
of him, ready to start work. He is wearing a grey dressing-gown over a
lemon-yellow silk waistcoat.

M.B.

Oil on canvas
52.5 x 43.3 cm
Frederiksborg
Museum

Johan Frederik Clemens, engraver

10 | Jens Juel 1745–1802
Jørgen Scheel 1718–1786

A very large proportion of the production of Jens Juel's studio
consisted of oval portraits. They were painted to a fixed design and
were relatively uncomplicated to complete. Often Juel himself painted
the face, while assistants took care of the costume and background.
The portraits of Scheel and his wife are among those for which Juel
took responsibility for all the details. Scheel was one of the wealthiest
men in the country and in his time had been painted by artists as
distinguished as Jean-Marc Nattier, Louis Silvestre the Younger and
Carl Gustaf Pilo. A man of such stature could not, of course, be
required to make do with one of the ordinary products of the Juel
'portrait factory'. The portrait of Scheel, who belonged to one of the
oldest noble families in the country, is one of Juel's best, an unusually
expressive painting of an elderly aristocratic gentleman. Scheel is
depicted as Knight of the Danish Order of the Elephant, a testimony to
his close relations with the royal house.

S.H.

Oil on canvas
72 x 58 cm
Inscribed on the
reverse: Painted by
Juel 1781
Gammel Estrup,
Jyllands
Herregårdsmuseum

11 | Jens Juel 1745–1802
Charlotte Louise Plessen 1720–1801

This painting is a pendant of the portrait of Jørgen Scheel. Even though the sitter is well-advanced in years, she has taken pains to be depicted in accordance with the latest fashion, including an exaggerated elaborately-high hair-style. She is displaying on her chest the order of *L'union parfaite* which was awarded as a particular personal appreciation to both men and women at the Danish court. The order was established by King Christian VI and Queen Sophia Magdalena in 1732 to commemorate their own happy marriage, and it was awarded until the Queen's death in 1770.

S.H.

Oil on canvas
72 x 58 cm
Inscribed on the reverse: Painted by Juel 1781
Gammel Estrup, Jyllands Herregårdsmuseum

Jørgen Scheel, Royal Equerry

Charlotte Louise Plessen, wife of Jørgen Scheel

12 | Jens Juel 1745–1802
Joseph Greenway died 1821

Joseph Greenway was one of the Englishmen who sailed under the
Danish flag of convenience in the 1780s, partly because of the
difficulties of movement of British ships during the American War of
Independence, and partly to circumvent the East India Company's
monopoly in England of trade with India. He became a Danish citizen
in 1785. His ship, originally *Neptunus*, was rechristened *Enrum*
(Solitude), after the estate of that name in Vedbæk, north of
Copenhagen, belonging to his Danish agent, Conrad Fabritius de
Tengnagel.

Jens Juel's portrait of Greenway is linked to the English tradition of
placing the subjects in a relaxed attitude out-of-doors, in contrast
to the Danish portrait tradition with its often very formal posing.
It was probably the subject's own wishes which lay behind the
Gainsborough-inspired arrangement. A painting such as this may
well have contributed to the breakthrough of outdoor portraits in
Denmark. The most notable examples are in fact to be found in the
ship-owning and trading circles of which Greenway was a member,
most conspicuously in Juel's major painting of the Ryberg family from
the middle of the 1790s. Juel was a talented landscape artist and was
therefore especially well-qualified to develop the outdoor portrait. But
it was not just a matter of new trends in art. It was in precisely the
same circles that the Rousseau-inspired ideas about primitive virtues
and nature had had their strongest impact.

It is tempting to suggest that the romantic landscape is the garden
at *Enrum* with its view over Øresund, out to the ships which formed
the basis for Captain Greenway's prosperity.

S.H.

1788
Oil on canvas
79.8 x 99 cm
Inscribed: J. Juel
pinxit Hafniæ 1788
National Gallery,
London

Captain Joseph Greenway, merchant

13 | Jens Juel 1745–1802
Thomasine Gyllembourg, née Buntzen 1773–1856

c. 1790
Oil on canvas
61 x 47 cm
Frederiksborg
Museum

In 1790, at the age of sixteen, Thomasine Buntzen married the controversial writer Peter Andreas Heiberg. The marriage was not harmonious. Heiberg neglected his young wife and failed to take her seriously on an intellectual level. On the other hand she was fêted by the many celebrities who came to their home. She fell in love with a Swedish baron, C.F. Gyllembourg, and refused to accompany her husband into exile. They were divorced, and after a dramatic row, their little son, later to become the poet Johan Ludvig Heiberg, was placed with foster-parents. She married Gyllembourg and after his death kept house for her son. At the age of fifty-three she made her literary debut quite by chance when her son solicited her help because he was short of material for his literary magazine *Københavns Flyvende Post* (Copenhagen's Flying Post). During the following decades she wrote a number of short stories and novels under a pseudonym. Today her books mainly retain their significance on account of their descriptions of life and social mores in Copenhagen, especially between the two sexes, during the first half of the nineteenth century. However, her range of ideas is linked more to eighteenth-century Enlightenment than nineteenth-century Romanticism. Together with her daughter-in-law, the actress Johanne Luise Heiberg (cat. no. 41), she played her part in establishing the Heibergs' home among the leading circles of the Copenhagen bourgeoisie.

The picture is a pendant to the portrait of Peter Andreas Heiberg.

S.H.

14 | Jens Juel 1745–1802
Peter Andreas Heiberg 1758–1841

In his satirical writings Peter Andreas Heiberg ridiculed the political
and social principles upon which Danish society was based:
absolutism, the awarding of orders and decorations, the system of
rank and precedence, and officialdom. His poetic satire on a royal
wedding beginning "Orders and decorations are hung on idiots" led to
a fine for "rash criticism of His Majesty the King's practice of awarding
honours". Heiberg was an unconditional supporter of the French
Revolution. He characterized the execution of Louis XIV in a poem as
"his just reward". In his home he received exiled Swedes who had been
accused of complicity in the murder of Gustav III of Sweden in 1792.
The fact that the government usually turned a blind eye to the writings
of this convinced republican was prompted by a wish to avoid direct
conflict with public opinion.

Heiberg's position was weakened in the course of the 1790s when
people became increasingly critical of France and the Revolution.
Freedom of the press was restricted in 1799 and that same year
Heiberg was banished for having offended foreign heads of state. He
went to Paris and was given a post in the French Foreign Ministry.
After the fall of Napoleon he lost his job and lived for many years in
miserable conditions.

Jens Juel's picture was painted on the occasion of Heiberg's wedding
in 1790. Being a revolutionary, he let himself be painted without a wig.

S.H.

c. 1790
Oil on canvas
60.5 x 47 cm
Frederiksborg
Museum

Thomasine Gyllembourg, née Buntzen, writer

Peter Andreas Heiberg, poet and playwright

15 | Jens Juel 1745–1802
William Duntzfelt 1762–1809

c. 1800
Oil on canvas
105 x 82 cm
Frederiksborg
Museum

Duntzfelt grew up in the Danish colonies of Tranquebar and Frederiksnagore in India. He was employed by the Danish Asiatic Company, but also engaged in trade between Europe and India on his own account. At the age of twenty-nine he moved to Denmark and became the partner and son-in-law of Copenhagen's biggest shipowner, the Dutch-born Frederik de Coninck. Together they exploited the favourable business conditions for neutral trading during the wars between England and France, and succeeded in building up enormous – by Danish standards – trading empires. The French occupation of the Netherlands had ruined Dutch trade, and for a period Copenhagen replaced Amsterdam as Northern Europe's trading centre for colonial products such as sugar, coffee and tea. However, the 1807–14 war with England put an end to the so-called 'palmy days' of Denmark's overseas trade and Duntzfelt suffered great losses.

The picture is undated, but was probably painted around 1800.

S.H.

William Duntzfelt, merchant and shipowner

16 Jens Juel 1745–1802
Lorentz Lassen 1756–1837

Lorentz Lassen distinguished himself at the Battle of Copenhagen in
1801 by defending the block-ship *Prøvestenen* (Touchstone) until it
was shot to pieces by the English attackers. His bravery earned him a
gift from the women of Denmark and Norway. He is depicted in naval
uniform with the gold medal "Courage Defends", which the king
awarded to all who had excelled themselves during the battle. During
the war of 1807–14 against Great Britain he was in command of coastal
defences in the south of Norway.

Jens Juel's picture emphasizes the contemporary opinion of Lassen
as a brave and conscientious soldier, simple and unsophisticated. The
picture was painted in 1802, shortly before the artist's death.

S.H.

1802
Oil on canvas
69 x 53.5 cm
Frederiksborg
Museum

Rear-Admiral Lorentz Lassen

17 | Bertel Thorvaldsen 1770–1844
Self-portrait

The sculptor Bertel Thorvaldsen was a handsome man with regular features and clear blue eyes. In his youth he had thick, curly hair, and when he was an old man it was still thick, but long and white, as can be seen from the portrait from 1839 (cat. no. 33) and in a daguerreo-type from 1840. Thanks to his good looks and fame, over a hundred portraits were made of Thorvaldsen in his lifetime.

This self-portrait was drawn in 1810, the same year as Thorvaldsen modelled his first portrait bust of himself, which had been com-missioned by the Danish diplomat and art collector Hans West for the Royal Danish Academy of Fine Arts, where it can still be seen. The bust, colossal in format, shows Thorvaldsen with a wavy mane of hair and the eyes bored out. "So expressive, such a likeness, Sire! 'Tis the gaze of Jupiter, and it is flesh!" wrote West to the President of the Academy, later Christian VIII. The self-portrait drawing, in which the head is turned to look at the mirror, was possibly made in connection with work on the bust.

M.B.

1810
Black chalk on paper
23 x 18 cm
Signed: Thorvaldsen 1810
Ny Carlsberg Glyptotek, Copenhagen

Bertel Thorvaldsen, sculptor

18 Bertel Thorvaldsen 1770–1844
Ida Brun 1792–1857

In 1797 Bertel Thorvaldsen arrived in Rome, which became his home for the next 41 years. In the early years in Rome he worked mainly on statues and reliefs of classical subjects such as the major statue of Jason begun in 1800. This bust of Ida Brun is one of his earliest female portrait-busts. Ida Brun sat for it in 1809, while she was visiting Rome. Her mother then commissioned it in marble. The young woman is shown completely at rest. Her facial features are simplified, and the hair, drawn up, is held in place, according to the demands of fashion at that time, by a head-band with a bow, creating an eloquent contrast with the smoothness of the face.

Ida Brun was the incarnation of all that was classical. She was the daughter of a prosperous Danish merchant, Constantin Brun, and of a poet, Frederike Brun. With her mother she travelled all over Europe singing and performing sketches at courts and among artists and poets. Goethe, Chateaubriand and Canova were all enraptured by the talented young girl. Madame de Staël lauded her in *De l'Allemagne* in 1810, while Lamartine and A.W. Schlegel wrote poetic tributes to her. In 1816 Ida Brun married the Austrian diplomat Count Louis Philippe de Bombelles.

The Danish poet Adam Oehlenschlæger described her thus: "Ida was a delightful girl, blonde, pale, as well-formed as a nymph, with an oval, perfectly-shaped head, beautiful hair and a face so cheerfully friendly that she impressed us all, even though her blue-green eyes did not sparkle with passion."

M.B.

1809
Marble bust
H. 56.5 cm
The Thorvaldsen
Museum,
Copenhagen

Ida Brun, mimic and performer

19   Bertel Thorvaldsen 1770–1844
Christoffer Wilhelm Eckersberg 1783–1853

In 1814, the young painter Christoffer Wilhelm Eckersberg had painted in Rome a splendid portrait of Thorvaldsen which he donated to the Royal Academy of Fine Arts in Copenhagen. In return for this portrait Thorvaldsen modelled a bust of Eckersberg shortly before the painter left Rome after having studied there for three years. Eckersberg only sat for the sculptor for a couple of hours. Just as had been the case with the self-portrait bust from 1810, Thorvaldsen chose the herm form, but the Eckersberg herm has neither the vigour nor the penetrating 'gaze of Jupiter' of the Thorvaldsen bust. Eckersberg's physiognomy hardly lent itself to a portrait in the grand style. His round face and mild expression, combined with the fact that the bored-out pupils seem to be too high for the gaze to catch the spectator's eye, prevent the portrait from having the same appeal as many of Thorvaldsen's other portrait busts. However, a comparison between the marble version and the original model reveal that the former is an idealization of what the sculptor originally saw.

M.B.

1816
Marble bust
H. 53,5 cm
Inscribed:
Eckersberg pittore
THORVALDSEN.
FACEVA. ROMA.
LI MAGGIO
MDCCCXVI
Thorvaldsen
Museum,
Copenhagen

Christoffer Wilhelm Eckersberg, painter

20 | Bertel Thorvaldsen 1770–1844
Prince Friedrich of Augustenborg 1800–1865

Prince Friedrich, later called the Prince of Nør, belonged to the Augustenborg ducal family, whose history goes back to 1651. His mother was a Danish princess, the result of a relationship between Queen Caroline Mathilde (see cat. no. 6) and Johann Friedrich Struensee, physician-in-ordinary to Christian VII. The prince and his elder brother came to Rome in 1819 on their Grand Tour and it was on this occasion that they both had their portraits done by Thorvaldsen, who also acted as the princes' guide in the city.

Thorvaldsen has given a fine rendering of the young man's regular features, full lips and curly hair. Instead of a bared breast he is depicted with a draped shoulder cape, undoubtedly inspired by Roman portrait busts which Thorvaldsen had seen in the Museo Capitolino.

The prince and his family subsequently suffered tragic fates. On the outbreak of the first Schleswig war the prince and his brother sided with Prussia, which resulted in banishment and the loss of all their possessions in Denmark in 1848. The Augustenborg ducal family died out in 1931.

M.B.

1819
Marble bust
H. 70.5 cm
Thorvaldsen
Museum,
Copenhagen

Prince Friedrich of Augustenborg

21 | Christoffer Wilhelm Eckersberg 1783–1853
Sophie Hedvig Løvenskiold, née Adeler 1795–1859,
and her daughter Bertha Henriette Frederikke

Eckersberg studied abroad for six years, first in Paris (1810–13) and
then in Rome (1813–16). This portrait of a noblewoman with her child
was painted the year after his return to Denmark. The relief-like
arrangement of the figures and the mother's rigid, distant gaze are
typical of Eckersberg. Despite the intimate depiction of the mother,
one hand protectively holding her three-year-old daughter, who is
placed on a table in front of her mother with her legs in her mother's
lap, there is certain stiffness in the representation. Both mother and
child are obviously posing for the painter. The child in the white dress
is represented sweetly, but without sentimentality. The plasticity of
the figures, the clear and equally distributed light and, in particular,
the intense blue colour in the dress, reveal what Eckersberg had
learned from his teacher, the French painter Jacques-Louis David.

M.B.

1817
Oil on canvas
62.5 x 51.5 cm
The Royal Museum
of Fine Arts,
Copenhagen

Sophie Hedvig Løvenskiold and her daughter Bertha Henriette Frederikke

22 | Christoffer Wilhelm Eckersberg 1783–1853
Johan Gunder Adler 1784–1852

Adler was one of the Christian VIII's closest advisers during his brief reign as king of Norway in 1814 and of Denmark from 1839 until 1848. He drafted a constitution for Norway and took part in negotiations aimed at a Swedo-Norwegian union under Marshal Bernadotte that same year. On Christian's accession to the throne Adler became his private secretary and, behind the scenes, organized on the king's behalf a very comprehensive programme of financial support for those loyal sectors of the press that were expected to defend the government's policy.

The picture is typical of Eckersberg's benevolent approach. As the Danish art historian Bente Skovgaard has pointed out, Eckersberg seldom took any notice of the sitter's 'inner life'. According to the artist's records the picture was commenced on 26 January 1832 and completed on 22 February. On 31 January Eckersberg noted in his diary: "Prepared to paint Adler, but he did not come, so the day was wasted."

S.H.

1832
Oil on canvas
63.5 x 50 cm
Inscribed: E. 1832
Frederiksborg
Museum

Johan Gunder Adler, the King's private secretary

23 | Christen Købke 1810–1848
Jens Andreas Graah 1787–1873

Only rarely did Christen Købke undertake official portraits. The commission to paint Jens Andreas Graah was an exception. The portrait
was intended to be hung in the town hall of Hjørring in North Jutland,
where it still remains.

In his splendid red uniform tunic, a sable at his side and a rolled
document in his hand, this senior civil servant stands erect, staring
directly at the viewer. The austere, frontal placing of the figure against
a neutral brown background is straightforward, but also masterful.
The high format of the canvas emphasizes the monumental appearance of the figure. The prefect's face is weather-beaten, his hair is
grizzled and black shadows indicate beard growth. The embroideries
on the collar and cuffs, together with the decoration on his breast,
form the picture's only decorative features.

M.B.

1837–38
Oil on canvas
138 x 93 cm
Municipality of
Hjørring, Denmark

Jens Andreas Graah, prefect

24 | Christian Albrecht Jensen 1792–1870
Cathrine Jensen, née Lorenzen 1796–1874

C.A. Jensen painted his wife many times, but never with greater intensity and tenderness than in Frederiksborg Museum's portrait from *c.*1825–26. One senses inspiration from Raphael, whose works Jensen frequently copied during travels in Germany and Italy.

Cathrine Lorenzen was the sister of Peter Hiorth Lorenzen, one of the leaders of the Danish North Schleswig movement. In contrast, Jensen, who himself came from Schleswig, supported the German Schleswig-Holsteiners, as did his wife. This was one of many cases where nationalist sympathies split families in this country where Danes and Germans had previously lived side by side without major problems. The growth of nationalism also caused the disintegration of the cosmopolitan Danish-German élite culture which had been associated with the court in Copenhagen for centuries. Jensen became one of the victims of these developments when, as a result of the nationalist conflict, he lost his circle of customers in Copenhagen.

S.H.

c. 1825–26
Oil on canvas
63 x 51.5 cm
Frederiksborg
Museum

Cathrine Jensen, wife of the artist Christian Albrecht Jensen

25 | Emilius Ditlev Bærentzen 1799–1868
The Winther Family

The family picture was a favourite genre among the bourgeoisie in
Denmark during the 1820s and 1830s. Everyday situations in the
home, sometimes with an anecdotal content, were depicted with
meticulous accuracy on small canvases whose modest format made
them suitable for hanging on the walls of the unostentatious living-
rooms of those with money to spend. The first Danish art historian,
Niels Laurits Høyen (1798–1870), who was both a professor at the
Royal Academy and an influential art critic, specifically recommended
pictures of this type. As he wrote in 1838:

1827
Oil on canvas
70.5 x 65.5 cm
National Gallery of
Scotland

> Everyday life, even its most ordinary incidents, also the
> surroundings, even if they be not what we call picturesque,
> afford the artist an opportunity to display genuine artistic
> endeavour.

During the following years, Høyen's patriotic programme was to
become even more explicit. He encouraged artists to cultivate a
Danish range of subjects, paint Danish landscapes, Danish history
and the everyday lives of the urban as well as the rural Danish
population, declaring that "even the everyday life of the present
belongs to history".

Bærentzen's conversation piece from a middle-class Copenhagen
home can be located precisely. The spire of St Nicolai Church in the
centre of the city is visible outside the window. The Winther family are
shown engaged in two forms of activity: on the right, drinking coffee,
and on the left, playing with a puppy. Bærentzen, who was a pupil of
C.W. Eckersberg, painted several pictures of this type and was also
much in demand as a portrait painter. In 1838 he set up a lithographic
workshop which existed until 1874. He had become acquainted with
the new lithographic technique during a stay in Paris (1831–32), and
his workshop initiated, amongst other things, the mass production of
portraits of the celebrities of the day – a Danish pantheon – in the new
medium.

M.B.

The Winther Family

26 | Albert Küchler 1803–1886
Hans Christian Andersen 1805–1875

The first time Hans Christian Andersen sat for his portrait was in
Rome in the winter of 1833–34, but he was not entirely satisfied with
the picture painted by his countryman, Albert Küchler. In particular,
he complained about the thinness of his moustache – he would have
preferred a more pronounced confirmation of the manly adornment
he had acquired on his journey south. Moreover, he felt the portrait
was not sufficiently 'soulful'.

Andersen's reservations were no doubt due to the fact that Küchler's
picture differed from the normally very sympathetic manner in which
sitters were presented in traditional Danish portraiture. But it is
actually a very charitable picture. Wrapped up in a fur collar, stand-up
shirt-collar and neckcloth, the normally restless Andersen radiates
self-assurance, an almost dandy-like arrogance emphasized by the
slightly screwed-up eyes.

Küchler occupies a special place in Danish art on account of his
links with the German Nazarenes in Rome. Eckersberg wrote to him
that he had let himself be tempted by a certain 'Germano-Catholic
practice'. Eckersberg was thinking of Küchler's art, but the description
applies to Küchler's personal development. He converted to
Catholicism, was admitted to the Franciscan Order and became a
monk at the S. Bonaventura Monastery on the Palatine Hill.

S.H.

1833–34
Oil on canvas
25,5 x 20 cm
Frederiksborg
Museum

Hans Christian Andersen, writer

27 | Christian Albrecht Jensen 1792–1870
Herman Ernst Freund 1786–1840

The sculptor Herman Ernst Freund was born in Bremen in Germany. He came to Denmark at the age of eighteen and was admitted to the Royal Academy of Fine Arts in Copenhagen in 1809. Freund worked as an assistant in Thorvaldsen's studio in Rome and after Thorvaldsen was the leading Danish sculptor of the period. Freund introduced Nordic mythological figures into the art of sculpture. His Ragnarok frieze, depicting the last struggle of the Nordic gods, was intended as a counterpart to Thorvaldsen's Alexander frieze in the Quirinale Palace in Rome. With this work Freund had hoped to outshine his teacher. It was intended for Christiansborg Palace, but never completed; it was destroyed by fire in 1884.

Freund's home in Copenhagen, decorated in the Pompeian manner, including painted furniture and klismos chairs in the antique style, launched a new vogue in interior decoration.

Here he has been painted by the friend of his youth, C.A. Jensen, in Rome in 1835, wearing the garb of an artist: black beret and a shirt with broad white collar under an open-necked smock. The portrait has been painted quickly with thick brush-strokes, face to face with the sitter. Jensen's very small portraits, such as this one and cat. nos. 28, 29, 30, were much in demand.

M.B.

1835
Oil on copper
20 x 13.2 cm
The Royal Museum
of Fine Arts,
Copenhagen

Herman Ernst Freund, sculptor

28 | Christian Albrecht Jensen 1792–1870
Bernhard Severin Ingemann 1789–1862

C.A. Jensen's picture of the poet Bernhard Severin Ingemann shows the subject as very youthful in appearance in spite of his 30 or so years; it was painted in 1818 or 1819, in Rome, where Jensen painted a series of small portraits of some of the Danish artists, poets and academics who were staying in the Eternal City at that time.

Ingemann was already an established poet by then, but it was after his return from Rome to Denmark that his popularity as a writer grew in earnest. With Walter Scott as his model, in the 1820s and 30s he published a number of major historical novels which shaped the very romantic notions of the Middle Ages in Denmark that prevailed for several generations. The novels are no longer popular reading-matter; on the other hand, Ingemann's songs and hymns are still sung in schools and churches. In the course of time he came to prominence as a great national poet.

S.H.

Oil on copper
18 x 11.5 cm
Inscribed: Iensen
[R]om 181..
Frederiksborg
Museum

Bernhard Severin Ingemann, poet

Christian Albrecht Jensen 1792–1870

Mathilde Therese von Irgens-Bergh 1793–1861

The portrait of Mathias Friis von Irgens-Bergh's wife, Matilde Therese, is a small masterpiece. She is fashionably dressed exclusively in black and white. In a splendid hat decorated with feathers and with her head turned slightly in relation to her body, she is at one and the same time coquettish and reserved. Fragile white rows of pearls are her only decoration. The black and white colouring is only broken by the light, warm tones of the carnation and the brown hair. The refined simplicity is an inheritance from the classical portrait-art of the sixteenth and seventeenth centuries.

C.A. Jensen's portraits from this period, with their colouring, the light virtuoso technique and the lively characterization, made a deep impression on some of his younger contemporaries. Others, with the art historian N.L. Høyen in the forefront, criticized his free and temperamental brush-work, and called him unacademic. Gradually the commissions dwindled and from about 1850 onwards he completely stopped painting. It was not until the present century that his qualities again began to be appreciated. Among his 400 portraits there are several which in painting technique and in the rendering of personality bear comparison with the works of Frans Hals.

H.L.

1824
Oil on canvas
24.4 x 19.8 cm
Signed: Iensen 1824
Royal Museum of
Fine Arts,
Copenhagen

Christian Albrecht Jensen 1792–1870
Mathias Friis von Irgens-Bergh 1786–1828

1824
Oil on canvas
24.4 x 19.8 cm
Inscribed:
Iensen 1824
Royal Museum of
Fine Arts,
Copenhagen

C.A. Jensen opted single-mindedly for a career as a portrait painter, deciding not to complete the last part of his course at the Royal Academy of Fine Arts, which covered history painting. Instead, he chose to travel in order to extend his knowledge of portraiture. He went first to Berlin, and then to Dresden, where he stayed for some time, working as a copyist, and where he met several of the people who later became his customers. The goal of the journey was Rome, where he stayed for three years; from there he made many visits to Florence. He became familiar with the latest trends in the field, using small formats and intimate rendering of facial features, strongly influenced by the Renaissance concept of portraiture.

When Jensen returned to Copenhagen to settle there in the early 1820s, the contacts he had made on his travels began to bear fruit. He was given several large commissions by the royal house and the aristocracy, and at the same time he also took up the small format portraits which had been so highly prized in Rome.

One such work was the portrait of Mathias Friis von Irgens-Bergh, who had been Jensen's landlord in Dresden. Irgens-Bergh was a lawyer and made a career as a diplomat. After demonstrating his abilities during the Congress of Vienna he was appointed *chargé d'affaires* in Dresden. Jensen's portrait depicts him as a slightly formal and reserved man in a black coat, white stock and choker-collar. The red ribbon of the Order of the Commander's Cross of the Prussian Red Eagle provides a delicate colour-highlight in this otherwise black and white portrait.

H.L.

Mathilde Therese von Irgens-Bergh, wife of Mathias Friis von Irgens-Bergh

Mathias Friis von Irgens-Bergh, diplomat

31 Christian Albrecht Jensen 1792–1870
Hans Christian Ørsted 1777–1851

1842
Oil on canvas
66.5 x 51.5 cm
Signed:
C.A. Jensen 1842
Frederiksborg
Museum

The physicist Hans Christian Ørsted is especially known for having demonstrated that an electric current can cause the deflection of a compass needle, but he also exercised great influence in his day on the intellectual life in Denmark on account of his view that a confirmation of 'the spirit' – or reason – in nature was to be found in the natural sciences.

C.A. Jensen painted Ørsted's portrait for the Royal Portrait Collection at Frederiksborg in 1842. It is one of his most expressive pictures, although the creative process was by no means easy. His patron and well-wisher, Christian VIII, interfered and asked to have the picture changed in several respects. Jensen was also obliged, on the king's orders, to repaint other portrait commissions for Frederiksborg. This does not necessarily indicate that Christian VIII was dissatisfied with the quality, but he was aware that Denmark's leading art critic, Niels Laurits Høyen, was extremely ill-disposed towards Jensen. From an artistic viewpoint, Jensen's broad brushstrokes were the stumbling-block. The king's decision to intervene may have been prompted by a wish to avoid public discussion about the acquisitions made by the Royal Portrait Gallery.

S.H.

Hans Christian Ørsted, physicist

32 | Christian Albrecht Jensen 1792–1870
Anton Frederik Tscherning 1795–1874

The painting of A.F. Tscherning, officer and politician, is one of
C.A. Jensen's most outstanding portraits. It was exhibited at the Royal
Academy of Fine Arts in 1851 and must date from one of the preceding
years. This is of great interest. Tscherning was Minister for War in
1848, and was thus the man who organized the Danish war effort
against the Schleswig-Holstein rebels. Jensen, who was himself born
in Schleswig, supported the Schleswig-Holstein insurgents.
Tscherning, in his choice of artist, must have set aside nationalist
prejudices.

   Tscherning himself was also a rebel, but in a different way.
Politically he was linked with what were known as the 'Peasants'
Friends', and he agitated for a much further-reaching democratization
of society and of the political system than the prevailing National-
Liberal thinking could tolerate. This aroused opposition when during
the war he extended conscription to cover not only peasants but also
the young bourgeoisie. In 1866 he tried in vain to persuade King
Christian IX not to sign the revised national constitution, which he
considered to be a step backwards for democracy.

S.H.

c. 1851
Oil on canvas
68.5 x 53.5 cm
Frederiksborg
Museum

Colonel Anton Frederik Tscherning, Minister of Defence

33 | Christian Albrecht Jensen 1792–1870
Bertel Thorvaldsen 1770–1844

No Dane has ever received greater homage than Thorvaldsen on his return to Denmark in 1838 after more than 40 years in Rome. The whole of Copenhagen was astir, and he was taken in a carriage to the Royal Academy of Fine Arts, where he was called out on the balcony – according to his own account – "in the very same way as when the Pope gives his blessings". His portrait was painted the following year by C.A. Jensen for the Royal Portrait Collection at Frederiksborg. The sculptor is wearing the uniform of the Roman San Luca Academy, a black cape and decorations in the style of Soviet marshalls of a later era. In addition to the Cross of the Order of the Dannebrog, his international standing is confirmed by his Russian, Prussian, Austrian, Bavarian, Württembergian and Neapolitan decorations.

It was not easy for Jensen to portray such a monumental figure. Although the face is full of character it does not really come into its own right in the formal arrangement, for the sartorial splendour and magnificent decorations somehow steal the picture. The sitter might just as well be a minister or an officer were it not for Thorvaldsen's own Nemesis figure on the right-hand side of the picture – a tangible expression of his art, but also of his awareness of the dangers of overweening pride.

S.H.

1839
Oil on canvas
139 x 100 cm
Signed: Aetatis
Suae 68 Anno
1839/C.A. Jensen
pinxit Hafniae.
Frederiksborg
Museum

Bertel Thorvaldsen, sculptor

34 | Johan Vilhelm Gertner 1818–1871
Bertel Thorvaldsen 1770–1844

On 24 March 1844 Bertel Thorvaldsen died of a heart attack while he was sitting in the Royal Theatre in Copenhagen. Gertner made his drawing of him the day after, and the portrait seems to confirm a statement made by Thorvaldsen's friend and patron Baroness Rigmor Stampe, that "never has there been so beautiful a corpse; his features were unchanged, and even his colouring looked healthy and strong".

The sculptor's coffin was placed in Frue Kirke (The Church of Our Lady, Copenhagen's cathedral), for four years until 1848, when it was moved to a tomb built for it in the courtyard of the Thorvaldsen Museum. Thorvaldsen had presented his great art collection to the town of his birth, Copenhagen, which in the years 1839–48 erected a museum building in the centre of the town, close to Christiansborg Castle, to house the magnificent gift. The Thorvaldsen Museum, which was designed by the architect Michael Gottlieb Bindesbøll, is a unique work in Danish architecture with its polychrome exterior and interior decoration.

M.B.

1844
Pencil on paper
26.4 x 21.5 cm
Inscribed:
J. V. Gertner,
f. Charlottenborg
d. 25. Marts 1844
Frederiksborg
Museum

Bertel Thorvaldsen, sculptor

35 | Wilhelm Marstrand 1810–1873
Søren Kierkegaard 1813–1855

There are very few depictions of the physical appearance of the philosopher Søren Kierkegaard from his own lifetime. He never agreed to be painted or sculpted. Kierkegaard lived all his life in the centre of Copenhagen and was a well-known figure in the city streets. He was easy prey for cartoonists: thin, with a crooked, almost deformed body, a high forehead, bristly hair, heavy eyelids and a wide mouth. The philosopher Hans Brøchner described his impression of his first meeting with Kierkegaard, when the latter was 23, in 1836. He had

1870
Indian ink on paper
33.3 x 17.7 cm
Inscribed: S.
Kirkegaard
Frederiksborg
Museum

> something irregular about his whole frame, and a massive hair-style. His hair stood up in a frizzy crest almost six inches above his forehead, and he looked strangely confused on account of it.

From his manner and appearance Brøchner gained the impression that Kierkegaard was a shop-assistant.

After Kierkegaard's death, Wilhelm Marstrand, who had doubtless seen his notable figure in the streets of Copenhagen, drew several striking sketches, including this well-known caricature from 1870. It depicts the wandering philosopher alone and with his umbrella under his arm as his inseparable companion, whether in rain or sunshine. It is not an unsympathetic caricature. In a striking way it reflects the disharmony between head and body, between spiritual capacity and physical frailty.

M.B.

Søren Kierkegaard, philosopher

36 | Johan Thomas Lundbye 1818–1848
Peter Christian Skovgaard 1817–1875

Johan Thomas Lundbye was one of the finest landscapists among the
painters of Denmark's so-called 'golden age'. His love of Danish nature
and history was expressed in small as well as monumental landscapes
in which ancient dolmens or medieval churches and castles were
often major features.

   Here he has painted his red-bearded friend and artist colleague, the
painter P. C. Skovgaard – also a brilliant landscapist – wearing an
artist's smock and a black skullcap. The solemn, reserved Skovgaard
has turned his head and is gazing obliquely out of the picture, past the
viewer. The face is modelled by the light, which falls in from behind.
Lundbye died at the age of thirty, killed by an accidental shot in 1848
when he volunteered for service in the first Schleswig war.

M.B.

1843
Oil on canvas
27.5 x 20.5 cm
Signed with a
monogram and
'1843 Veiby'
Frederiksborg
Museum

Peter Christian Skovgaard, painter

37 | Christen Købke 1810–1848
An old peasant woman

Christen Købke's depictions of people are perceptive, and his keen sense of colour and composition enabled him to create portraits of great beauty. The identity of this old peasant woman is unknown. The painter has registered all the details of her distinctive, weather-beaten face as well as the various patterns and textures of the fabrics. Despite the small format, the old woman's dark eyes and attentive expression, combined with the slightly turned head and neutral greyish background, make it a striking study of a human being. Only on a few occasions did Købke paint portraits on a large scale, such as that of Jens Andreas Graah (cat. no. 23).

M.B.

1832
Oil on canvas
31 x 27 cm
Randers
Kunstmuseum

An old peasant woman

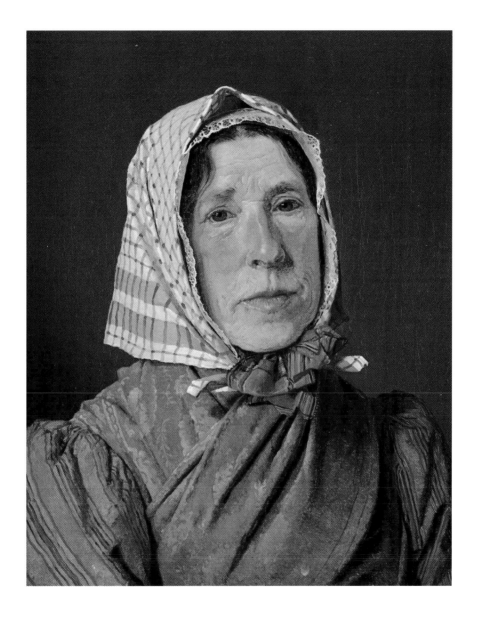

Johan Vilhelm Gertner 1818–1871
Laurids Engelstoft 1774–1851

Gertner is not among the best-known Danish artists, but his painted and drawn portraits are unsurpassed as regards their incisive psychological characterization, and taken together they constitute a fantastic collection of the personalities of Golden Age Copenhagen. This little painting of the elderly historian Laurids Engelstoft is no exception.

The picture was painted in 1846, but Engelstoft belongs to another age. As a historian he emphasized the importance of national history, but in contrast to the Romantic historians he never isolated the history of Denmark from its broader European context. He wrote as readily about Byzantium in the time of Justinian as about Denmark under Christian IV, and his works are characterized by general reflections on the history and cultural development of humanity, with clear evidence of influence from Holberg, Montesquieu, Gibbon and other great European historians from the eighteenth century. For Engelstoft, the pedagogical and character-forming significance of history was central; pedantic source-criticism was not his aim.

S.H.

1846
Oil on panel
26 x 29 cm
Inscribed:
I. Vilhelm Gertner.
pinx./1846
Frederiksborg
Museum

Laurids Engelstoft, historian

39 | Johan Vilhelm Gertner 1818–1871
Frederik VII 1808–1863

The painting shows Frederik VII standing on the deck of the naval ship *Danmark*, in admiral's uniform. The picture was a present from Frederik VII to the British ambassador, the Right Honourable Henry-Watkin Wynn, on his departure from Copenhagen in 1854.

Oil on canvas
113.8 x 71.5 cm
Frederiksborg
Museum

In March 1848, forced by the pressures of political developments, Frederik VII gave up the absolute monarchy, and his name is associated with the free constitution of 1849. The nationalist conflict between the Danes and the Germans within the Danish monarchy led in 1848 to the Schleswig-Holstein revolt. The Danes were victorious in military terms, but no solution to the problem was found. Any arrangement satisfactory in Danish eyes would presuppose a good relationship with the major powers, and Britain in particular was a target of appeal. Frederik VII's gift to Wynn should be seen in this context.

It was anger over the Schleswig-Holstein revolt which caused Frederik VII to give in to the demands of the National Liberal opposition for a free constitution, but his dislike of hard work and his mythomaniac tendencies would in any case have made it difficult for him to fulfil the role of absolute monarch. What he lost in political power he won back instead in popularity as a national rallying-point. On journeys around the country he demonstrated a great talent for winning personal support, and his motto "The people's love is my strength" was no empty phrase.

S.H.

Frederik VII, King of Denmark, reigned 1848–1863

40 | Constantin Hansen 1803–1880
The Constituent National Assembly of 1848

The picture is a study for the large picture of the Constituent National Assembly (338 x 500 cm) at Frederiksborg executed in 1860-64. Despite the monumental format it had been commissioned privately by a Copenhagen merchant named Alfred Hage, whose widow donated the picture to the Frederiksborg Museum in 1878. The idea for the picture came from the National Liberal politician Orla Lehmann, one of the major figures in the Constituent National Assembly, which prepared the Constitution of 1849.

1860–64
Oil on canvas
81 x 125 cm
The Folketing
(Denmark's
Parliament)

The picture was not intended as an exact representation of a historic situation. The event is interpreted in the light of the artist's own national and Christian ideals. In the front row he has placed the National Liberal politicians, to whom decisive importance is thus attributed for the change in the political system and the free constitution.

To the right in the picture, in front of the others, the painter has placed the man who suggested the painting, Orla Lehmann (in profile). Slightly to his right, but placed far back in the picture and sitting at a green-topped table or bar, is the clergyman and poet N.F.S. Grundtvig. The placing is apparently humble, but the vanishing point for the main lines of the picture is above Grundtvig's head. In this way the artist has indicated his support of Grundtvig's national and Christian ideas, which formed the ideological basis for Orla Lehmann and the activities of the National Liberals.

Historically, it is a case of manipulation, for it constructs a political and ideological agreement between Grundtvig and Orla Lehmann which did not exist in 1848, but which Lehmann, when the picture was painted at the beginning of the 1860s, wished to have as part of his historical posthumous reputation.

S.H.

The Constituent National Assembly

41 | Wilhelm Marstrand 1810–1873
Johanne Luise Heiberg 1812–1890

Johanne Luise Heiberg was the greatest Danish actress of the nineteenth century. She was married to the writer Johan Ludvig Heiberg, who had been spellbound when he saw her in her first stage performance aged only fourteen. He wrote a large number of plays with roles designed for her. He became Director of the Royal Theatre and in 1858, when he was the target of impassioned attacks concerning his management of the theatre, this could not fail to have an effect on her too, although she was otherwise a great favourite with the public. She followed her husband and left when he gave up his post. The following year she allowed herself to be persuaded, however, to return to the stage.

In the middle of the crisis in 1858 Wilhelm Marstrand was given the chance to paint the portrait which he had dreamt of for a long time, and which posterity has judged to be his most significant work. Johanne Luise Heiberg is painted full-length in a monumental style. Like a goddess of antiquity she is standing wrapped in a white shawl which clings closely to her figure in the plain black dress. She is gazing dreamily through the window at the view across the water. In his use of the window Marstrand evokes connotations of innumerable portraits from the Italian Renaissance.

With regard to the reception of the painting in 1859, in Johanne Luise Heiberg's autobiography, *Et Liv gjenoplevet i Erindringen* (A Life Relived in Memory), she writes that it aroused strong displeasure because the garments were so close-fitting. This was not considered appropriate at a time when the crinoline and farthingale were the height of fashion. The artist was disappointed that many criticized the portrait on the grounds that the actress looked too serious. To this he replied that seriousness had been the conscious aim. It was meant to give the painting historical significance by calling to mind the period in her life when a shameful injustice had forced her to leave her rightful occupation.

H.L.

1859
Oil on canvas
196.5 x 102 cm
Inscribed: WM 1859
Frederiksborg
Museum

Johanne Luise Heiberg, actress

Peter Severin Krøyer 1851–1909
Ferdinand Meldahl 1827–1908

42

Oil on canvas
87 x 68.5 cm
Frederiksborg
Museum

Ferdinand Meldahl was one of his generation's most influential architects. At the age of thirty-two he was entrusted with the task of rebuilding Frederiksborg Castle after the fire of 1859, a task which he carried out with brilliance. Together with the brewer Jacob Christian Jacobsen, founder of the Carlsberg Breweries, he was closely involved from 1877 onwards in the creation of the Museum of National History at Frederiksborg. He worked furthermore on the restoration of the country's two other most magnificent Renaissance buildings, Kronborg Castle and Rosenborg Palace, as well as restoring various manor houses in accordance with the principles established by Viollet-le-Duc. He was also an important town planner, establishing a green belt of parks around the medieval heart of Copenhagen when the city's old defence fortifications were pulled down in 1867. He was a professor of architecture, director of the Royal Academy of Fine Arts and author of several books on the history of architecture.

In 1882 P.S. Krøyer painted an excellent full-length portrait of this talented and self-confident man of the world, which is now in the Royal Museum of Fine Arts. The portrait exhibited here was executed that same year for the collection of artist portraits in the Royal Academy of Fine Arts. On the table can be seen a drawing of the Marble Church in Copenhagen, which was completed by Meldahl in 1894. This church, commenced in 1749, was later abandoned and subsequently became a ruin. It is Copenhagen's only domed church.

M.B.

Ferdinand Meldahl, architect

43 | Laurits Tuxen 1853–1927
Christian IX and Queen Louise 1818–1906 and 1817–1898

1883
Oil on canvas
109 x 131 cm
Frederiksborg
Museum

In 1883 Laurits Tuxen was commissioned to paint a large group portrait of the Danish king and queen surrounded by their children, sons-in-law, daughters-in-law and grandchildren, amongst whom were included King George I of Greece, Czar Alexander III of Russia and the Prince of Wales, later Edward VII of the Great Britain. The family was grouped in the large room opening on to the garden at Fredensborg Palace, where numerous family gatherings were held during the last decades of the nineteenth century.

Tuxen executed a number of separate studies for the figure groups, of which this is one. The artist has succeeded in portraying the king and queen gently and sympathetically. The brisk, brilliant brushwork, especially in the queen's black-and-red dress and in the jewellery and decorations, is characteristic of this artist.

The final group portrait was executed in a huge format (430 x 665 cm) for Christiansborg Palace in Copenhagen. Tuxen painted a smaller replica for Princess Alexandra of Wales to hang in Marlborough House in London. This was later transferred to Sandringham House, where it still is. The group portrait of the Danish royal family inspired Queen Victoria to have a similar family group portrait executed at Windsor Castle in 1887, her Golden Jubilee year. Other pictures painted by Tuxen for the English royal family include representations of events such as *The Marriage of the Duke and Duchess of York* in 1894, *The Marriage of Prince Carl of Norway and Princess Maud* in 1896, *A Garden Party at Buckingham Palace* in 1900 and three pictures of the coronation of Edward VII and Queen Alexandra in 1903.

M.B.

Christian IX and Queen Louise

44 Bertha Wegmann 1847–1926
Philip Julius Schou 1838–1922

Bertha Wegmann became one of the most important portrait-painters in Danish Realism in spite of the fact that as a woman she was excluded from studying at the Royal Academy of Fine Arts. Unlike many of the other women who aspired to be artists at that time, she had the good fortune to have her father's support. She first took painting instruction in private art schools and then travelled to Munich, where she studied history painting and portrait-painting from 1867 to 1881. In the years that followed she made many journeys to Paris, where she visited Léon Bonnat's studio. In 1882 she was awarded a gold medal at the Salon in Paris for a portrait of her sister, and the following year this also won her an exhibition prize at the Royal Academy of Fine Arts. At the same time she was elected as the first woman to join the plenary assembly of the Academy, and in 1887 she became a member. National and international honours were heaped on her, and she cultivated a large clientèle in bourgeois and aristocratic circles.

This portrait of the director of the Royal Copenhagen Porcelain Manufactory, Philip Schou, is typical of Wegmann's elegant portrait style. Slightly reserved in posture, but with a lively expression on his face, he is depicted leaning against a table. The picture is from 1888, when he was at the peak of his career. At that time there was a decisive renewal taking place at the factory; the new artistic director, Arnold Krog, introduced the underglazing technique which aroused great interest at the Nordic Exhibition in Copenhagen in 1888.

The following year Royal Danish porcelain received the Grand Prix at the World Exhibition in Paris. The porcelain was now world-famous and in the 1890s Philip Schou was able to open his own outlets for sale of Royal Danish porcelain in Paris, London and New York.

H.L.

1888
Oil on canvas
142.2 x 82.5 cm
Signed:
B. Wegmann
Frederiksborg
Museum

Philip Julius Schou, director

45 | Peter Severin Krøyer 1851–1909
A meeting of the Royal Danish Academy of Sciences and Letters, 1897

The most impressive of Krøyer's qualities is his virtuosity. Although he is perhaps best known for his paintings from Skagen, he was also one of the leading portrait-painters of his time. His many pictures of groups are of particular interest, since they portray both environments and personalities which influenced society and its development around the turn of the century. Bourgeois social events, both private and institutional, found in him their painter. He painted the industrial élite assembled in an electricity plant, the capitalists in the Stock Exchange in Copenhagen, and rendered the progress of medical knowledge visible in a group picture of the country's leading doctors gathered in the Finsen Institute. He also sought out industrial work-places, e.g. for a painting of the large smithy at the Burmeister & Wain shipyard in Copenhagen.

The period around the turn of the century was an era of greatness for Danish academic achievement and for the University of Copenhagen. The academic élite was portrayed by Krøyer in a painting of a meeting of the Academy of Sciences and Letters, an august institution established in 1742. In 1899 the Academy moved into a building of its own, erected by the Carlsberg Foundation. The meeting-room's decoration included Krøyer's monumental painting of the Academy's members.

The painting shown here is a sketch for that major painting, but there are divergencies in a number of details. In the centre of the picture, without any form of limelight, sits the patron of the Academy, the Crown Prince, later King Frederik VIII.

S.H.

Oil on canvas
71 x 136.5 cm
Inscribed:
S. Krøyer 1897
The Hirschprung
Collection,
Copenhagen

The Royal Danish Academy of Sciences and Letters, 1897

46 | August Jerndorff 1846–1906
Carl Jacobsen 1842–1914

Carl Jacobsen was the son of the founder of the Carlsberg Brewery, J. C. Jacobsen, the great philanthropist who established the Carlsberg Foundation, the Carlsberg Laboratory and the Frederiksborg Museum. The son followed in his father's footsteps. He became an equally talented brewer and possibly an even greater patron of the arts. In order to support art he founded the Ny Carlsberg Foundation, became an art collector on a grand scale and opened to the public his remarkable collections of antique Greek, Roman and Egyptian art and of modern French sculpture which are now housed in the Ny Carlsberg Glyptotek in Copenhagen.

In his brewery, Ny Carlsberg, he was responsible for the construction of several exceptional buildings which today are seen as outstanding works of nineteenth century industrial architecture. He enhanced the town of Copenhagen by presenting it with about 60 monuments and sculptures, one of which, *The Little Mermaid* – the work of Edvard Eriksen, 1913, based on one of Hans Christian Andersen's stories – has become the tourist emblem of Copenhagen.

The portrait is painted by August Jerndorff, who had also painted the official portrait of the father, J.C. Jacobsen, in 1886. Carl Jacobsen is depicted in exactly the same way as his father. He is standing in his study at a table with objects which characterize him as a brewer: a microscope, flasks, barley-grains, Louis Pasteur's book about beer-making, a plan of the brewery and labels for Ny Carlsberg lager. The green curtain beside the door in the background is a bold contrast to the otherwise muffled tones of the room's Bordeaux walls. Through the doorway there is a view of a room with a classical frieze. With its self-conscious attitude the portrait testifies to Carl's efforts, even here, to outdo his father.

H.L.

1893
Oil on canvas
166 x 113 cm
Inscribed: A. J. Pinx
1893
Carl Jacobsen
Ætatis suæ 51
Frederiksborg
Museum

Carl Jacobsen, brewer and patron of the arts

47 | Peter Severin Krøyer 1851–1909
Martin Nyrop 1849–1921
and Emil Jørgensen 1858–1942

After P.S. Krøyer had trained at the Royal Academy of Fine Arts in Copenhagen and then at Léon Bonnat's studio in Paris he became one of the main figures in the breakthrough of Realism in Denmark in the 1880s. As the favourite portrait painter of the time he depicted the leading Copenhagen industrial bourgeoisie in a new way. The striking portraits were executed with sweeping virtuousity in a rapid sketch-like painting technique distinguished by spontaneity and directness. As well as individual portraits Krøyer painted large group-portraits which bore the stamp of his ability to place the members of a large assembled group in apparently random postures, with the instantaneous element emphasized by the placing of some of the figures only half within the picture-frame.

Krøyer belonged to the circle of artists which gathered in the little fishing hamlet of Skagen at the northern tip of Jutland, where the light was strong on the sea and where there were many opportunities for outdoor painting. Here his painting acquired new facets after his marriage to the artist Marie Triepcke in 1889. She became the central point of a series of emotion-laden blue shore-paintings, in which the twilight atmosphere is an innovative interpretation of the long Nordic evenings.

The colour blue and outdoor painting lend qualities to this sketch of a painting for Copenhagen Town Hall of architect Martin Nyrop and his clerk-of-works, architect Emil Jørgensen, wearing a cap. Martin Nyrop designed the new Town Hall, a major work in the nationalistic Romantic style, built in 1892–1905 in red brick and richly decorated with imaginary figures in granite. One of these, a watchman-figure, can be seen behind the two subjects, who are caught in a working situation on the roof of the Town Hall, in the process of studying a drawing.

H.L.

Oil on canvas
68 x 92 cm
Signed: S. K. 1900
Frederiksborg
Museum

Martin Nyrop and Emil Jørgensen, architects

48 | Harald Slott-Møller 1864–1937
Anne Marie Carl Nielsen, née Brodersen 1863–1945

Harald Slott-Møller belongs to the group of artists who embraced Symbolism in the 1890s. The portrait of the sculptor Anne Marie Carl Nielsen was painted after Slott-Møller's first journey to Italy, and was inspired by his encounters with early Italian art. In a simplified form he accounts for the blonde, Nordic facial features of his subject. Her light blue eyes have the same colour as the sky of the background. The hair is a strangely stylized form of decoration, in that the upper part of the hair has been cut in relief into the panel on which the picture is painted. A couple of light touches on the hair highlight the relief. The red dress is effectively contrasted against the luminous blue sky.

Anne Marie Brodersen, who married the composer Carl Nielsen in 1891 and then took his name, was an artist in her own right. In 1889-90 she attended the Art School for Women in Copenhagen, since women could not be admitted to the Royal Academy of Fine Arts. She is known in particular for her realistic animal sculptures, but also carried out major works such as an equestrian statue of Christian IX in front of Christiansborg Palace. In 1939–40 her monument to her husband, in the form of an equestrian statue with a young man playing the flute, was erected in Copenhagen.

M.B.

1890
Oil on panel
59 x 42.5 cm
Odense Municipal Museums

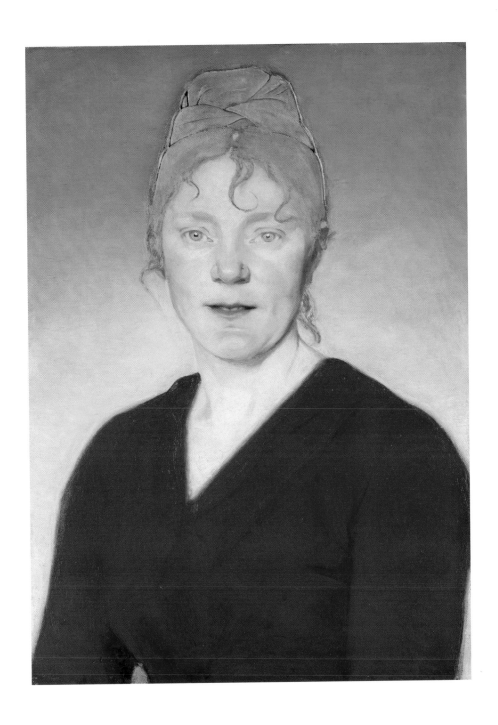

Anne Marie Carl Nielsen, sculptor

49 | Harald Slott-Møller 1864–1937
Helge Rode 1870–1937

Harald Slott-Møller's portrait of the poet Helge Rode is an example of harmony between painter and subject. Both became fascinated by Symbolism in the 1890s.

   Harald Slott-Møller had been among the founders of *Den frie Udstilling* (The Independent Exhibition) in 1891, but he soon decided to follow his own route, supported by his wife, who was also a painter; he went after an idealistic, beauty-worshipping style which was nourished by several visits to England, where he was drawn to the Pre-Raphaelites. This led to a break with the artists in *Den frie Udstilling* and a rejection of Naturalism with its exclusive cultivation of external reality. Symbolism demanded that ideas and emotions should be made visible in symbolic imagery. Slott-Møller and his wife became isolated in Danish artistic circles and were criticised for their 'literary' paintings. One of their supporters was Helge Rode. This portrait of him is a remarkable likeness. The narrow face with the large nose, the expressive eyes and the voluminous wavy hair are strikingly well-rendered. The poet's dreamy universe is hinted at in the distant blue hills of the background and the stars of the night sky.

H.L.

1907
Oil on canvas
80.5 x 69 cm
Frederiksborg
Museum

Helge Rode, writer

50 | Herman Vedel 1875–1948
Nina Grieg, née *Hagerup* 1845–1935

Herman Vedel's portrait study of the elderly lady with white hair is
gentle and beautiful. Vedel, who as a rule used a very limited scale of
colours in his portraits, has introduced here, by way of exception, a
very bright blue. Nina Hagerup was married in 1867 to the Norwegian
composer Edvard Grieg. She herself was both a singer and a pianist.
The sketch is a study for a double portrait of Nina Grieg and her sister.

M.B.

c. 1928
Oil on canvas
55 x 45 cm
Frederiksborg
Museum

Nina Grieg, pianist

Herman Vedel 1875–1948
F.C. Krarup 1852–1931

It is characteristic of Herman Vedel's portraits that he favours grey and
black colour-tones and makes use of the chiaroscuro technique, often
with considerable virtuosity. In spite of the distinctly painterly
qualities of his pictures he was rather underestimated by his own
times, and this is probably related to the fact that he earned his living
to a large extent from commissions for official portraits, including
some for the National Portrait Gallery at Frederiksborg. Current
renewed interest in portrait-painting as a genre seems to indicate
development towards a more perceptive evaluation, however.

Krarup was a respected theologian who attempted, with a point of
departure in Kant's epistemology, to situate theology and science
within a single coherent system.

S.H.

1930
Oil on canvas
70.4 x 52.7 cm
Frederiksborg
Museum

F.C. Krarup, clergyman

52 Julius Paulsen 1860–1940
Self-portrait

Together with Herman Vedel, Julius Paulsen was the last great portrait-painter of the old school in Denmark. He was a professor at the Royal Academy of Fine Arts from 1908 until 1920. His characterizations are sensitive, the glow of light and colour having an almost Rembrandt-like quality. In this unpretentious, yet extremely sophisticated self-portrait, the figure is seen against the light, which is reflected in the oval spectacle lenses. Like cat. no. 42, the self-portrait belongs to the series of painted artist portraits executed for the exhibition building of the Royal Academy of Fine Arts in Charlottenborg Palace. The collection, which consists of 109 portraits of artists executed between 1867 and 1945, was handed over to the Frederiksborg Museum in 1996.

M.B.

1912
Oil on canvas
86.5 x 68.5 cm
Signed: Jul. Paulsen
1912
Frederiksborg
Museum

Julius Paulsen, painter

53 | Herman Vedel 1875–1948
Knud Rasmussen 1879–1933

Knud Rasmussen, who had maternal ancestors from Greenland, lived during his boyhood in Greenland and put down the roots then of his lifelong love of that country and of the Greenlanders. In 1902–04 he took part in his first Greenland Expedition. His exceptional abilities as an Arctic explorer became evident. He was dauntless and energetic, spoke the Inuit language, had a sound sense of direction and was a gifted dog-sledge driver. In the period from 1912 to 1932 he was leader of seven Thule Expeditions to North-East Greenland, Arctic Canada and Alaska, and these supplied the background for pioneering research on the life and culture of the Eskimos.

Rasmussen's writing ranges across literary work, travel accounts, translations of Eskimo tales, legends and songs, and rigorous scientific contributions. He was made an honorary member of a number of geographical societies, and received many other honours, including honorary doctorates from the University of Copenhagen in 1924 and from St Andrew's University, Scotland, in 1927. In 1928 Frederiksborg Museum commissioned a portrait of him from the most skilful official portrait-painter of the time, Herman Vedel, who painted him clad in an anorak of reindeer-hide and with a long dog-whip wound round his hand.

H.L.

1928
Oil on canvas
79 x 65.2 cm
Frederiksborg
Museum

Knud Rasmussen, Arctic explorer

54 | Herman Vedel 1875–1948
Christian X 1870–1947

Christian X, the grandfather of the present Queen, was the son of
Frederik VIII and of the Swedish-born Queen Louise. In 1912 he
succeeded his father as king. He caused the most serious constitution-
al crisis the Danish monarchy has experienced since the end of the
absolute monarchy in 1848. In March 1920 he unilaterally dismissed
the Government, and Denmark was in fact without any government
for more than 24 hours. Nevertheless, Christian X was a respected and
well-liked monarch, and especially during the German Occupation of
Denmark from 1940 to 45 he enjoyed immense popularity as a symbol
of unity on his daily unescorted horse-rides through the streets of
Copenhagen.

Vedel's portrait-sketch was painted around 1929 as a preparatory
work for an official full-length portrait commissioned by the
Frederiksborg Museum for hanging in the Great Hall at Frederiksborg
Castle. The hall was equipped as a kind of potentate's gallery with full-
length portraits of Christian IX, his children and sons- and daughters-
in-law, including Edward VII and Queen Alexandra of Great Britain.
The spontaneously executed study is a small colouristic masterpiece.
The king's red dress uniform with the blue embroidered collar is
sketched with the same rapid broad brush-strokes with which the
orders and epaulettes are indicated. The shape of the head is moulded
by a strong light from the left and bluish shadows on the right side.

M.B.

1929
Oil on canvas
45.5 x 40.5 cm
Frederiksborg
Museum

Christian X, King of Denmark, reigned 1912-1947

55 | Vilhelm Lundstrøm 1893–1950
Ole Vinding 1906–1985

Vilhelm Lundstrøm is an outstanding representative of early Danish
Modernism. From 1916 he exhibited Cubist compositions and
sculptural objects. His abstract collages of paper, cardboard, metal
and diverse objects provoked animated debate, in which prominent
physicians took part with the purpose of condemning the artist and
his like-minded colleagues as mentally ill. From the 1920s onwards
Lundstrøm executed a large number of self-portraits and portraits of
friends, as well as large figure-paintings in a clear and strong
geometric style. In the years 1923-32 he lived in Cagnes-sur-Mer in
Southern France, where there was a small Danish colony of artists.
It was there that he painted the young journalist and author Ole
Vinding, who was later to become an outstanding advocate of French
culture and art in Denmark, and who had also, as early as in the 1940s,
been an enthusiastic champion of protection of nature and of animal
and plant life.

Lundstrøm's portrait of the 21-year-old journalist is a typical
example of this artist's simplified, monumental portrait-style, where
all unimportant details have been eliminated. Sigurd Schultz, a
prominent critic and later director of the Thorvaldsen Museum in
Copenhagen, described Ole Vinding's portrait in the following terms:
"In spite of the extraordinary simplification in this portrait of a young
man with a black cap, the total impression is lively, fine and soft – it is
really a portrait of a human being, not just a still-life painted from a
human figure".

M.B.

1927
Oil on canvas
100 x 81 cm
Inscribed: VL
Randers Art
Museum

Ole Vinding, writer

56 | Kai Nielsen 1882–1924
Dick Nelson 1880–1922

The sculptor Kai Nielsen came from Funen. With his exuberant love of
nature and his positive attitude to life he became an adjunct to the
group of artists known as the Funen group. In his art Naturalism
fought with Classicism, but he also managed to fuse several types of
style together and to give the result his own personal stamp. In his
youth he strove energetically to improve his physique by gymnastics
and sport, with the aim of instilling vitality into his sculptures, which
thus became a vivid appreciation of the naked human form.

Throughout his whole career Kai Nielsen sculpted portrait busts
which are characterized by his desire to depict the human being as a
type rather than as an individual. Several of his works are expressions
of homage to sporting life, especially wrestling and boxing. This
applies to the limestone bust of the 38-year-old boxer Dick Nelson. Its
outline has clear, economical lines, distinguished by simplicity and
severity, but also by uncompromising realism. Up from the roughly-
shaped base rises the neck, bearing the head with the brutal marks of
blows to the nose, mouth and ears. The sculpture was a gift to Karl
Madsen, art historian and director of the Royal Museum of Fine Arts.
In his letter of thanks Madsen described the bust as "the best of Kai's
many good busts... a truly classical masterpiece of modern sculpture".

H.L.

1918
Limestone bust
H. 49.5 cm
Inscribed: Til Hr.
Karl Madsen fra
Deres hengivne Kai
Nielsen. Julen 1918
Ny Carlsberg
Glyptotek,
Copenhagen

Dick Nelson, boxer

57 Adam Fischer 1888–1968
Eva la Cour born 1908

Adam Fischer belongs to the group of Danish artists who settled in
Paris for a protracted period. He arrived in 1913 and stayed for twenty
years. He was originally a painter, but in Paris quickly realized that he
wanted to be a sculptor. Cubism was in vogue, and he managed to
exhibit one of the few Cubist sculptures in Danish art before
becoming involved in 1918 with the reaction against Cubism started
by the Mexican painter Diego Rivera. Around 1923 Fischer came into
contact with the French sculptor Aristide Maillol, whose classically
inclined sculptures were to be of great importance to his later
development. It was probably Maillol who inspired him to take an
interest in archaic Greek sculpture. The bust of Eva la Cour, wife of the
poet Paul la Cour, is typical of his almost schematic form. Everything
unimportant has been eliminated; the model's clean-cut features
emerge softly, yet at the same time majestically.

H.L.

1935
Granite bust
H. 46 cm
Ny Carlsberg
Glyptotek,
Copenhagen

Eva la Cour

58 | Harald Giersing 1881–1927
Self-portrait

Harald Giersing went to Paris in 1907 to study painting and seek new ideas for the rebellion he was conducting against naturalism. He found inspiration for this in the work of Cézanne, Gauguin and the Neo-impressionists. In February he wrote to a friend in Denmark: "I am modestly painting portraits, most modestly self-portraits." In the course of his career Giersing painted around forty of these, not because he was specially absorbed in his own physiognomy but because his model was always at hand and cost nothing.

The self-portrait from 1909 belongs to the group of hypermodern (by Danish standards) portraits he executed after his stay in Paris. The artist has caught himself in the middle of an outburst with his mouth open and an inquiring expression. In this respect it is similar to another famous self-portrait in Danish art, Jens Juel's so-called 'gaping' portrait of 1767. But whereas Juel's expression was friendly and welcoming, Giersing's is rather superior – this is emphasized by the bold composition. He is displaced in relation to the middle of the picture, as if he were on his way into it. The lighting, which comes from above, is also unusual. The most illuminated parts, his forehead and blue-black hair, are the most carefully painted, while the remainder are characterized by broad brushstrokes in thin paint on a coarse priming. Traces of the pointillist style of painting inspired by Neo-impressionism are a typical outcome of his period in Paris. However, what his contemporaries found most striking at the time were his simplified forms, the emphasis on delineation and a restricted scale of colours in black and blue on a glazed, pale blue background.

H.L.

1909
Oil on compoboard
61 x 47 cm
Signed: HG 09
Randers
Kunstmuseum

Harald Giersing, painter

59 | Karl Isakson 1878–1922
   Astrid Noack 1888–1954

Karl Isakson was born in Sweden and studied painting at the Royal Academy of Fine Arts in Stockholm. However, he spent most of his working life in Denmark, interrupted by many visits to Italy, Berlin and above all Paris. In 1910 he was deeply absorbed by Cézanne. This was the introduction to a decade during which he strove to achieve perfect luminosity in his painting through the intensity of his colours. During this period he painted a series of pictures of female models in which the sensual is united with an aura of gentle chastity and purity.

Purity also characterizes his portrait of the sculptor Astrid Noack, painted around 1918. At the age of thirty, after having worked for a number of years as a woodcarver, Noack turned to sculpture. She soon joined the circle round the sculptor Adam Fischer in Paris, where she stayed from 1920 to 1932.

Isakson's portrait of this slight woman, her face shown in profile, was painted in the colours preferred by the artist in his last, late summer landscapes from Christiansø off the island of Bornholm in the Baltic. Here he came closest to Cézanne by using light tones of grey, blue, cool green and ochre that conjure up a world of purity. Her seated figure is imbued with an air of tranquillity that is also reflected in Noack's later sculptures. She developed a simple, pure form of expression that makes it difficult to place her within any 'ism'. With great naturalness, she achieved intimacy and monumentality at one and the same time.

H.L.

c. 1918
Oil on canvas
72.5 x 51.5 cm
Ny Carlsberg
Glyptotek,
Copenhagen

Astrid Noack, sculptor

60 | Sigurd Swane 1879–1973
Carl Nielsen 1865–1931

The dominating figure in the musical life of Denmark in this century is the composer Carl Nielsen, who grew up on the Danish island of Funen as one of a family of twelve brothers and sisters – he was a shepherd boy at the age of eight. However, his musical talent was evident and he was given financial support to study the violin and composition at the Conservatoire in Copenhagen.

His *œuvre* comprises six symphonies, chamber music, choral works and about 250 tunes for a series of popular Danish songs that served to make him particularly well-known and cherished. His autobiography *Min fynske Barndom* (My Funen Childhood) is one of the most charming books in this genre.

His portrait was painted by Sigurd Swane, who studied painting at the Royal Academy of Fine Arts at the time when the Symbolist and Late Romantic climate prevailing there round the turn of the century. In 1907 he went to Paris with his friend, the painter Harald Giersing. Their encounter with Matisse, Derain and Rouault, who used bright, contrasting colours applied to the canvas with quick, broad brushstrokes, proved to be of decisive importance to Danish painting and led to the breakthrough of modernism.

The portrait of Carl Nielsen from 1931 is marked by a strongly colouristic idiom. The 66-year-old composer is depicted against a strong red background that endows him with the youthful vitality, creativity and willpower that had made him what he was.

H.L.

1931
Oil on canvas
63.8 x 52.7 cm
Odense Municipal
Museums

Carl Nielsen, composer

61 | Johannes Bjerg 1886–1955
Peter Vilhelm Jensen-Klint 1855–1930

The architect P.V. Jensen-Klint is an outstanding figure in Danish architecture. His buildings had their roots in his comprehension of national building traditions, particularly from the Middle Ages and the baroque period, and through the whole of his professional career he laid stress on the material qualities of brick.

His main work, the Grundtvig Church, designed in the years from 1913 onwards and built between 1921 and 1940, is sited on one of the highest points in Copenhagen and is a monumental paraphrase of the concept of the Danish village church. The tower in particular is remarkable, especially because of its gable with ornamental recesses inspired by late Gothic architecture. With a colossal nave and flying buttresses, all in yellow brick, the church achieves the monumentality of a cathedral. Jensen-Klint himself called it an outsized village church. The quality of the craftsmanship and the architectural details came to have great significance for later brick architecture in Denmark.

The sculptor Johannes Bjerg portrays the architect in grey-black polished granite, as rock-rugged and monumental as the church. In the abundant hair and distinctive beard the curling locks are indicated by incised wavy lines. The simplified garments consist of an artist's smock with a yoke and vertical folds falling from it. The expression on the face, with its distinctive features, is a smiling one which resembles certain archaic sculptures. Greece was the major source of inspiration for Bjerg, as it also was for many of the French sculptors he met in Paris in the years 1911-14.

H.L.

1916-17
Granite bust
H. 59.5 cm
Frederiksborg
Museum

Peter Vilhelm Jensen-Klint, architect

62 | Jens Ferdinand Willumsen 1863–1958
Gustav Philipsen 1853–1925

1919
Oil on canvas
61.5 x 50.5 cm
Signed: J. F. W.
5 Septbr. 1919
Frederiksborg
Museum

In 1919, when a new portrait of a politician was to be painted for the Copenhagen Town Hall, the choice fell on the artist J. F. Willumsen, because it was hoped that he would produce a more lively portrait than those of the previous mayors, who all looked like "men in black coats who could just as well have been undertakers".

J. F. Willumsen was originally schooled in Naturalism, but after studying in Paris, Brittany and Spain he became one of the most conspicuous figures in the breakthrough of Symbolism in Denmark around 1890. His *Women from Brittany* from 1890 features a stylization of form, colour and line which is related to Paul Gauguin's style of expression. A journey to France and Spain in 1910–11 became the introduction to a new development in Willumsen's art. The strong sunlight and the orgy of colour made a deep impression on him.

In the portrait of Gustav Philipsen complementary colours are juxtaposed in their strongest contrasts. The bold yellow background contrasts with the lilac suit. The face is predominantly in yellowish nuances apart from some strong red shadows which are reflections from the red veranda where the sitting took place. The painting is a preparatory work for a double portrait in which Mayor Jacob Marstrand, who is shown frontally, is actually the principal figure. The representation of the subsidiary figure is so interesting, however, with the subject's sideways posture, leaning back, that the picture can be seen as a portrait in its own right.

H.L.

Gustav Philipsen, politician

63 | Jens Ferdinand Willumsen 1863–1958
Johannes Poulsen 1881–1938

J.F. Willumsen painted another double portrait. In this case, however, it is the same person who is featured in the double role as producer and actor.

Johannes Poulsen was a member of a famous acting family and had a brilliant career in the Danish Royal Theatre. He was renowned as a character-actor of genius, with a vast knowledge of costume, and for his exceptional ability to create very different faces.

J.F. Willumsen depicts him in the role of Henry VIII in the play *Cant* by the young poet and clergyman, Kaj Munk, at the moment when, as producer, he steps out of the role and lets down the mask in order to subject his character to further scrutiny. Johannes Poulsen's remarkable interpretation of a Renaissance man, coarse, harsh and bawdy to the point of foolishness, but also acutely quick-witted and authoritative, contributed to Kaj Munk's first success as a playwright. Among Willumsen's portraits this picture is a characteristic demonstration of his ability to find a form which was uniquely appropriate to the subject.

H.L.

1933
Oil on canvas
140 x 192 cm
Signed: J. F.
Willumsen 1933.
The Royal Theatre,
Copenhagen

Johannes Poulsen, actor

64 | Henry Heerup 1907–1993
Liva Weel 1897–1952

1945
Oil on canvas,
mounted on
masonite
60 x 61 cm
Signed: Heerup 45
Frederiksborg
Museum

Liva Weel was a famous stage personality. Her musical and comic talent blossomed first in the medium of musical revues. Later she played a range of character parts in various Copenhagen theatres. When she worked together with the architect and author Poul Henningsen, who wrote clever revue texts for her, Liva Weel's interpretations of ballads rose to the highest level of art. During the German Occupation her soulful and warm renditions of songs expressing the Danish attitude to the Germans made her virtually a national symbol.

Henry Heerup's paintings and sculptures are unlike anything else in Danish art. He was neither abstract nor naturalist, but worked in the border zone between dream and reality. He made frequent use of easily accessible symbols – heart, cross, wheel or rainbow – often incorporating them into compositions as pure arabesques. He used clear unblended colours and was fond of colour symbolism. In his art the heart was always red. The portrait he painted of Liva Weel in the last year of the war is illustrative of his approach. Here the warm radiance of the actress is conveyed by giving the face the form of a heart. This form is reiterated in the curves of the breasts. The figure is composed of simplified geometric shapes, from the triangular mouth to the similarly triangular configuration of the body. The contours, as always in Heerup's art, are strongly defined, and the paint is applied in a thick layer. The subject's powerful stage aura is represented in the form of bluish-green wavy stripes.

H.L.

Liva Weel, actress and music hall artiste

65 | Fritz Syberg 1862–1939
Johannes Vilhelm Jensen 1873–1950

c. 1932
Oil on canvas
63.3 x 98 cm
Frederiksborg
Museum

Fritz Syberg was one of the artists in the 'Funen group', named after their place of origin, the island of Funen, where they painted rolling countryside, sun and summer and the wind sweeping over the fjord and the sea. As outdoor artists they combined an impressionistic approach with a realistic attitude to their everyday surroundings. In 1907 these artists became the target of strident criticism from the Symbolist Harald Slott-Møller, in particular for their choice of themes, which he found superficial and extrinsic. One of the supporters of the Funen group, in what came to be known as the 'peasant-painter feud', was the writer Johannes V. Jensen. A warm friendship then developed between the Funen painters and the poet.

In 1906 Fritz Syberg had painted *At Lunch,* inspired by a poem of that name from Johannes V. Jensen's first epoch-making collection, *Poems,* 1906. In that painting Syberg stressed the reality of the homely fare by using an impasto brush technique which gave a copious texture corresponding to Jensen's pioneering prose. Jensen was the founder of Modernism in Danish poetry, but he also wrote novels and tales from his home region, travelled far and wide in the world sending back brilliant journalistic reports, and became an ardent fan of modern American culture. In 1944 he received the Nobel Prize for Literature.

Fritz Syberg's portrait of Johannes V. Jensen, which was probably painted in 1932, is dominated by everyday realism. The subject is sitting in a brown chair wearing yellow-striped pyjamas and leaning his head on a white pillow. In spite of the informal and homely situation the author is endowed with an aura of intellectual literacy in the gleam of acute perception penetrating the spectacle lenses. The portrait is painted with a light, sketch-like technique, using thinned, transparent oils, inspired by the water-colour technique of which Syberg was an undoubted master. The hasty, similarly sketch-like composition ensures for Fritz Syberg a place in early Danish Modernism.

H.L.

Johannes Vilhelm Jensen, writer

66 | Olaf Rude 1886–1957
Queen Ingrid born 1910

Olaf Rude belonged to the group of painters who were strongly
influenced, in the years before the First World War, by French art, and
by Picasso in particular. Rude's compositions had features of Cubism,
but were seldom purely abstract. In his younger days he painted
mostly family members and friends, but did not embark on actual
portrait commissions. It was only later that he became a popular
portrait-painter, working with strong and simple coloured surfaces,
often in strictly frontal figure compositions, as in this portrait of
Queen Ingrid from 1952.

The Swedish-born princess, mother of the present Queen of
Denmark, was married in 1935 to the Danish Crown Prince, who
became King Frederik IX in 1947. The portrait came into being in
connection with the commissioning of official portraits of both the
King and the Queen for Frederiksborg Museum. The choice of the
previously avant-garde artist may seem surprisingly bold. In spite of
the official nature of the task set, the artist has managed to create a
portrait in which the artistic quality and the striking characteristics of
the Queen's distinct personality are united. In addition to the painting
shown here, Rude completed a larger, similarly frontal three-quarter-
length portrait of Queen Ingrid, which belongs to the Frederiksborg
Museum. The artist died before he could paint the portrait of the King.

M.B.

1952
Oil on canvas
73 x 60 cm
Her Majesty Queen
Ingrid

Her Majesty Queen Ingrid

67 | Rie Nissen 1904–1988
Karen Blixen née *Dinesen* 1885–1962

Karen Blixen's writing includes a large amount of autobiographical material, especially from the years she spent in Kenya, 1914–1931. She was one of those artists in whose works personal experiences are interwoven with myths. She loved to be photographed, and she used photography very consciously as a medium through which she could build up her image. The series of portraits taken by Rie Nissen in 1952 form a special group among the many photographs of Karen Blixen. In this portrait the writer is dressed up as Pierrot, the *commedia dell' arte* figure, which is traditionally a male role. She is thus consciously playing on androgyny by appearing in this frivolous costume. The photographic session in Rie Nissen's studio seems to have been an enchanted interlude. The photographer described the situation in her memoirs in the following terms:

> The costume suited her fantastically well, and she became deeply involved in the role of Pierrot, so that for the first time I discovered that there was also an actress latent in her. She particularly made much of the artfulness of her expression...

Another famous portrait by the same photographer from an earlier session, in fact in 1935, the year *Seven Gothic Tales* was published in Denmark, is a complete contrast: a black, mask-like portrait, as if the Great Reaper himself had come into the studio. The Pierrot and the black mask can be seen as two sides of the same coin. Blixen's motto 'By my mask ye shall know me' reverberates from both. The Blixen duality is thus given substance in her self-arranged photographs.

Rie Nissen was a central figure in the small cadre of Danish portrait photographers who pioneered the modern aesthetics of portrait photography, mainly influenced by the Bauhaus school.

T.T.

1952
Gelatine silver print
37 x 27 cm
Frederiksborg
Museum

Karen Blixen, writer

68 | Kay Christensen 1899–1981
Karen Blixen, née Dinesen 1885–1962

Karen Blixen stepped into the literary limelight in 1934 with the publication, under the pseudonym Isak Dinesen, of *Seven Gothic Tales*, and received great public acclaim. As a woman from an old landed upper class, she reached back in her stories to a romantic pre-bourgeois world and narrative technique. A strange, mysterious veil hangs over her, a kind of mask, through which she speaks directly into a contemporary context where the situation of women and of art are not the least significant themes. While the first book's tales are dominated by role-play, masks and mysterious turns of fate, *Winter's Tales*, from 1942, is to a greater extent a book about unexpected happiness and fatalistic acceptance. Between those two books came the autobiographical *Out of Africa*, in 1937, about a woman who came, who saw and who conquered, and then through defeat arose again as a narrator of stories of men and women.

Kay Christensen, who was commissioned by Frederiksborg Museum to paint Karen Blixen in 1955, was an artist with great imaginative qualities. In Danish art he was a loner whose imagery was characterized by delicate refinement, daring and expressive force. His main theme came to be that of the woman whose dreams and longings blend together with her surroundings in a beauty-seeking, dreamlike form. His personages find themselves in a place between dream and reality. The paintings are often dominated by one single colour, a red or a blue-green. It is also characteristic of his works that they include stylized exotic flowers and leaves.

All these elements are present in the depiction of Karen Blixen. Her fragile figure is loosely sketched on a grey-brown background on the left side of the picture. Under the yellow hat the face is visible as a pale mask with dark deep-set eyes. In her hand the indispensable cigarette is just discernible. To the right looms the mantelpiece, with flowers and clock, appearing out of dreamlike mists which hint at the universe from which her stories arose.

H.L.

1956
Oil on canvas
81 x 116.7 cm
Signed on the reverse:
Sunday 24 July 1955
– Kay Christensen
Frederiksborg Museum

Karen Blixen, writer

69 Anna Maria Lütken <small>born 1916</small>
Rudolf Broby Johansen <small>1900–1987</small>

Rudolf Broby Johansen was a writer and art-historian without any formal education. In 1922 his first collection of poems, *Blood*, was published, and it was immediately impounded on the grounds that it was blasphemous and pornographic. He wrote innumerable articles and books on art, politics and films. He was one of the most important interpreters of art of his time.

Anna Maria Lütken, with her expressive way of painting and harsh colours, has caught the personality of the disrespectful and argumentative critic of society and of art. His intense gaze especially discloses his fiery temperament. The portrait is unusual in its form. The head, which is larger than life-size, fills most of the painted surface. Lütken painted Broby Johansen three times. She was a pupil of Vilhelm Lundstrøm (see cat. no. 55) among others, and her art is mainly concerned with the human form.

M.B.

1971
Oil on canvas
100.5 x 91 cm
Hjørring Art
Museum

Rudolf Broby Johansen, writer and art historian

70 Knud Nellemose 1908–1996
Steen Eiler Rasmussen 1898–1990

Steen Eiler Rasmussen was an architect, town planner, professor of architecture, social commentator and writer. He was one of the most distinguished proponents of architecture in his generation. In 1934 his book on London was published; it was later re-issued in various editions, under the title *London: The Unique City*. From 1924-68 he was attached to the Royal Academy of Fine Arts as a teacher, and from 1938 he was Professor of Architecture there. In 1947, when he was in Britain, he was appointed Honorary Royal Designer for Industry by the Royal Society of Arts, and he was also Honorary Corresponding Member of the Royal Institute of British Architects. The lectures he gave as Lethaby Professor of Architecture at the Royal College of Art in 1958 were published as a book with the title *Experiencing Architecture* in 1960.

Nellemose sculpted a large number of exceptional portrait-busts and a few statues. Particularly in his depictions of sports figures he excelled in his fine ability to present complicated patterns of movement. He applied clay in lumps and left the surface uneven with clear traces of his working technique. This is also the case in this bust of the 87 year-old architect, who is represented in a toga befitting a Roman sage. In another example, which belongs to the Royal Academy of Fine Arts, Rasmussen is seen with bare shoulders.

M.B.

1985
Bronze bust
H. 54 cm
Signed: Nellemose
Frederiksborg
Museum

Steen Eiler Rasmussen, architect

71 | Kurt Trampedach born 1943
Vincent Lind born 1925

This portrait of Vincent Lind has been executed with extreme boldness, if one takes into account that the subject is a man of the cloth and the painting was commissioned to be hung in a cathedral. What is striking is the composition's simple frontality. The triangular form of the face is held up by the white circle of the ecclesiastical ruff, and the black and white surfaces of the vestments contrast with the fiery-red background. The paint is applied thickly on the canvas, almost like congealed lava, and in some places the artist has scratched and scraped at the colours to give the surface a pronounced texture. It is not only in its colouring that this portrait of the Lutheran bishop is striking, however. The face is endowed with an almost demonic quality which is characteristic of Trampedach, who has worked in particular with self-portraits and often transfers features from his own physiognomy to his other subjects.

M.B.

1990–91
Oil on canvas
104.5 x 75.5 cm
Inscribed: 'Biskop Vincent Lind Chilardico Borda 1990–1991' and 'Trampedach 1990–91'.
St Knud's Cathedral, Odense

Vincent Lind, Bishop of Funen

72 | Rigmor Mydtskov _{born 1925}
Queen Margrethe II _{born 1940}

This photograph was taken at Amalienborg Palace in Copenhagen on 18 February 1972. The young Queen is in mourning following her father's death and yet has to pose for the first official photograph in connection with her accession to the throne.

   The fact that it is the Queen who is the subject of Rigmor Mydtskov's portrait is evident not just from the exquisite jewels and the long dark-blue dress, but also from the subject's posture and from the formal profile. From among the many royal portraits of the Queen this will probably emerge as the most official. The icon status of this portrait was accentuated by the fact that it was used by Andy Warhol in his series 'Reigning Queens' from 1986.

T.T.

1972 (1992)
Colour photograph
after colour
negative
98.8 x 78.1 cm
Frederiksborg
Museum

Her Majesty Margrethe II, Queen of Denmark

73 | Niels Strøbek born 1944
Mogens Wahl 1918–1986

The portrait of Mogens Wahl, who was chairman of the board of
directors of the Frederiksborg Museum, was painted at the museum's
request. To emphasize the official nature of the commission the artist
decided to paint the Queen's private secretary in uniform and wearing
his decorations. He is striding, briefcase in hand, through the rooms of
the royal palace on his way to a meeting with his employer, Queen
Margrethe. However, the picture tells us more than this. Among the
papers can be seen some which refer to Wahl's former term as
Denmark's ombudsman, or representative of the Danish government,
in the Faroe Islands, a post which he held from 1961 to 1972. It was
created in 1948, when the Faroes became a self-governing community
within the Danish kingdom. A sheet of music from Mozart's 14th
piano concerto in E flat major indicates Wahl's interest in music.

M.B.

1986
Oil on plywood
114 x 72 cm
Signed: Strøbek
1986
Frederiksborg
Museum

Mogens Wahl, private secretary to Her Majesty the Queen

74 | Rigmor Mydtskov <small>born 1925</small>
Queen Margrethe II <small>born 1940</small>

Rigmor Mydtskov is masterly in the use of subtle colours. Her compositions are isochromatic, using a limited tone-range illuminated in different ways. The fact that she takes inspiration from the Old Masters is clearly evident in the official portrait of Queen Margrethe from 1972 (cat. no. 72) in which the pale bluish background is modulated with colour shading worthy of Pilo. This private portrait of the young Queen is one of a series of four, and was not made public until recently. It was taken with the same background as the official portrait, but the blue sky and the white clouds seem here to contain a stronger suggestion of infinite space. According to the photographer: "The Queen was still wearing black, but was not weighed down by grief."

The Queen is undoubtedly photogenic and during portrait sessions she evidently works cooperatively with the photographer. Throughout more than 25 years, Rigmor Mydtskov has demonstrated her understanding of how to capture the Queen's public image and to project it to her subjects. In 1986 Mydtskov was awarded the title 'Personal Photographer to Her Majesty the Queen', a title which no other photographer in Denmark has ever had.

T.T.

1972 (1997)
Colour photograph
from colour
negative
60.7 x 48.2 cm
Private collection

Her Majesty Margrethe II, Queen of Denmark

75 | Preben Hornung 1919–1989
Poul Verner Hansen born 1909

The portrait of Poul Verner Hansen, dean of Copenhagen's cathedral, is a study in black-and-white. The composition is strict, all inessential details having been eliminated. Hornung once declared:

> In reality I am a colourist, that's all I really am. It's where my strength lies. That is why I paint in black-and-white. Every time I paint with colours I have to abandon it. It becomes chaotic.

Predominantly a non-figurative painter, it was not until the last decade of his life that Hornung turned to portraiture. In his portraits he found ample opportunity to vary figure and colour in an arrangement involving a person in the same way as he had done hitherto in his abstract art. Among his official portraits are three of Queen Margrethe: a representation of the seated monarch in delicate green executed in 1981 for the Military College; a portrait wearing the chivalric costume of the Order of the Garter in black, white and red painted in 1983 for The Queen's Regiment, Canterbury; and finally, the somewhat controversial, full-length portrait in a blue dress against a white background painted for the Great Hall in Frederiksborg Castle in 1985.

M.B.

1984
Tempera on canvas
98 x 94 cm
Vor Frue Kirke (The Church of Our Lady), Copenhagen

Poul Verner Hansen, dean

76 | Pia Schutzmann born 1940
Erik Dal born 1922

Pia Schutzmann studied graphic art at the Royal Academy of Fine Arts, but since the beginning of the 1980s she has concentrated increasingly on portrait painting. Her portraits are characterized by the refinement of her colouring and the textural effect of her technique. They take form after many sittings, during which she appraises her sitter with a critical, curious eye. Not until genuine contact has been established does she accept a portrait commission. Her portraits are quiet, almost reticent, yet she has a knack of striking precisely the right note. This portrait is a typical example. Dr Erik Dal was administrator of the Danish Society of Linguistics and Literature from 1974 to 1991. He is shown seated, holding a book, apparently pondering over what he has just read without concern for either the artist or us. Erik Dal was chairman of the Royal Danish Society of Sciences and Letters from 1988 to 1994 and the portrait was executed for the learned society's premises in Copenhagen.

M.B.

Oil on canvas
87 x 65 cm
Signed:
Schutzmann
The Royal Danish
Society of Sciences
and Letters,
Copenhagen

Erik Dal, scholar of literature and linguistics

77 | Peter Martensen born 1953
Poul Hartling born 1914

Poul Hartling is a theologian and originally the principal of a college of
education until he became a politician. From 1968 to 1971 he was
Denmark's Foreign Minister and from 1973 to 1975 Prime Minister.
He ended his career as the UN's High Commissioner for Refugees
from 1978 until 1985.

Peter Martensen is one of the young Danish artists who have
dedicated themselves to reintroducing the human being into art. For
preference he paints almost monochrome pictures of people with
uniform, neutral faces in a space bathed in a diffuse, mysterious light.
He calls them 'spectator pictures'. The portrait of Poul Hartling, which
was painted for Denmark's National Portrait Gallery, is also almost
monochrome. The artist has succeeded in presenting a discreet yet at
the same time penetrating characterization of the 83-year-old
statesman, who radiates both tranquillity and authority.

M.B.

1996
Oil on canvas
110 x 95
Frederiksborg
Museum

Poul Hartling, theologian and prime minister

78 | Niels Strøbek born 1944
Red Dress

Niels Strøbek has cultivated a precise, neo-realistic style with dogged consistency for over thirty years in still lifes, landscapes, and portraits, in the course of which he has developed a steadily increasing mastery of his technique. He is much in demand as a painter of commissioned portraits but has also used his wife as a model in a number of studies from life. He often lets her appear twice in the same picture to show contrasting states, views or temperaments: a dressed and an undressed figure, a profile and an *en face* portrait, a cold and a sensual woman. In this portrait of a beautiful, mysterious woman in a red dress he has combined the subject's passion and reserve in the same figure and, by means of strong colours and a low angle, achieved a striking pictorial effect.

M.B.

1991
Oil on canvas
mounted on
masonite
76 x 57 cm
Nordjyllands
Kunstmuseum,
Aalborg

Red Dress, portrait of the artist's wife

79 Jørgen Boberg born 1940
Poul Christian Matthiessen born 1933

Poul Christian Matthiessen was formerly Professor of Demography at
Copenhagen University; since 1993 he has been Chairman of the
Board of Directors of Carlsberg Brewery and Chairman of the Board of
the Carlsberg Foundation. It is in the last-mentioned capacity that he
agreed to have his portrait painted by Jørgen Boberg for a meeting-
room in the distinguished mansion in Copenhagen where the Carlsberg Foundation is housed, along with the Royal Danish Academy of
Sciences and Letters.

1994
Acrylic and oil on
masonite
94 x 70 cm
The Carlsberg
Foundation

The portrait commission was to some extent limited, in that the
portrait had to be incorporated into panelling in a directors' meeting-
room where there is a whole gallery of portraits of the chairmen of the
foundation since 1876.

Boberg has chosen a traditional portrait format, in that he has
represented the subject sitting with his hands resting on the arms of a
chair, in the actual room for which the portrait is designed. As in the
portrait of Klaus Rifbjerg (cat. no. 80) the artist is here hinting at a
world outside the closed room. Parallel to the figure, on the wall
behind, one of the professor's predecessors in the post is visible, and
through the window there are the bare branches of a tree seen through
the blue-green Copenhagen mist. The blue tone and the sombre
colouring, which are typical of the artist, are enlivened only by the
subject's patterned tie.

M.B.

Poul Christian Matthiessen, Chairman of the Carlsberg Foundation

80 | Jørgen Boberg born 1940
Klaus Rifbjerg born 1931

Klaus Rifbjerg is a prominent and very productive writer of poems, novels, plays, and scripts for television and films. In addition, for the last forty years, he has been an enthusiastic participant in political and cultural debate in Denmark.

    Jørgen Boberg tends mostly to paint his artist colleagues, but he has also carried out more official commissions such as cat. no. 79 and this portrait, which was commissioned by the National Portrait Gallery at Frederiksborg. He prefers high, narrow formats and likes to place the subject strictly frontally in a dark, undefined space. Boberg's portrait art is characterized by technical perfection combined with the ability to fasten on a striking psychological characteristic. The realistic mode of painting nevertheless acquires a surreal dimension in the blue-green colour range which is a special element in Boberg's work. The plasticity of the shape of the writer's head and the rigorous frontality lend the picture a certain monumental weight in spite of the fact that it is a man in a denim shirt and casual green trousers that we have in front of us. The grapes on the table imply that the portrait was painted in Italy, where the artist has taken up residence.

M.B.

1994
Oil on masonite
103.5 x 64 cm
Frederiksborg
Museum

Klaus Rifbjerg, writer

81 | Thomas Kluge born 1969
Queen Margrethe II born 1940

Queen Margrethe has undoubtedly been portrayed more frequently
than anybody else in Denmark. Since her accession to the throne in
1972, more than a score of painters have painted her, foreigners as
well as Danes. Some of the portraits have been intended for the family
circle, others for a wider public. The Queen places herself at the
disposal of artists without interfering in how they set about their task.
This has resulted in a series of widely differing portraits, but probably
only Rigmor Mydtskov, photographer by appointment to HM the
Queen of Denmark, has succeeded in capturing all the many facets of
the Queen's personality (cf. cat. nos. 72 and 74).

Thomas Kluge's portrait of the Queen is a private picture. It was
commissioned by the Danish Chamber of Commerce as a wedding
present for the Queen's younger son and daughter-in-law, who were
married in November 1995. Kluge is a young, self-taught artist who
exhibited for the first time in 1994. The Queen sat for him on only two
occasions. In addition, he used photographs. He has not concerned
himself about the sitter's status but instead concentrated on creating a
portrait of the human being, devoid of any form of external finery; the
woman portrayed radiates the dignity she possesses by virtue of her
personality, not her office. Kluge gets as close to the true character of
his sitters as he can without revealing them mercilessly.

M.B.

1996
Acrylic on canvas
50 x 50 cm
Their Royal
Highnesses
Prince Joachim and
Princess Alexandra

Her Majesty Margrethe II, Queen of Denmark

82 | Torben Eskerod born 1960
Jytte Hilden born 1942

Jytte Hilden is a Social-Democrat politician. Since 1978 she has been a
Member of Parliament; from 1993 to 1996 she was Minister of Culture,
and now she is Minister for Research. Her energy and alertness are
clearly evident in this portrait. The raised nose and the sly look testify
to vigilance and indicate her ability to capture the attention of her
adversaries. The camera lens is less than half a metre from the
subject's eyes, and it requires cooperation on the part of the subject to
achieve a close-up shot of this kind.

    Since the middle of the 1990s Torben Eskerod has portrayed a
number of Danish politicians using the same technique of critical
inspection.

T.T.

1994
Gelatine silver print
50.7 x 40.8 cm
Frederiksborg
Museum

Jytte Hilden, graduate engineer and politician

83 | Rigmor Mydtskov <small>born 1925</small>
Suzanne Brøgger <small>born 1944,</small> and *Fleur Asmussen* <small>born 1929</small>

This double portrait of two cousins, later called 'Venetian Intrigue', was included in the exhibition *Homo Decorans* in the Louisiana Museum of Modern Art in 1985. The portrait is the result of a 'professional game' engaged in by the two subjects with the jewellery-designer Torben Hardenberg and the photographer. The actual point of departure was a situation in which the author Suzanne Brøgger was supposed to be the story-teller, while Fleur Asmussen and the others listened. The atmosphere of fantasy was heightened by the wearing of silk kimonos, dramatic make-up, and elaborate hair-styles with exotic hair-ornaments created for the occasion. From there the game progressed to an abstract composition with faces, necks, shoulders and the draped kimonos. The large perspex hair-ornaments look like hats.

Rigmor Mydtskov says of the subjects:

> They are both wonderful women to photograph, because even though both are no doubt aware of the effects they are creating, they both still have a special modesty in the camera-situation – a sense of 'don't come too close to me'.

Beginning in 1973 with the publication of *Fri os fra kærligheden* (Free us from Love), Suzanne Brøgger has written many novels, with partly autobiographical content, illustrating the many phases of the Women's Movement throughout the 70s, 80s and 90s.

The picture is experienced as a double portrait, but because of the similarity of the subjects it is also like a portrait with a *doppelgänger*. The photographer, who herself declares that she is always rehearsing being honest without being boring, has here created a new version of the Golden Section: the blue right-angled triangle is enclosed in the red semi-circle.

T.T.

1985
Colour photograph
from colour
negative
99.5 x 69.7 cm
Private collection

Suzanne Brøgger, writer, and *Fleur Asmussen,* graphic designer and writer

84 | Tove Kurtzweil born 1938
Lars von Trier born 1956

Filmdirector Lars von Trier was photographed in 1983 immediately after his breakthrough with the film *Elements of Crime* (1982). He studied at the Danish Film School from 1979 to 1982, and since then has worked on films and in television. His films tend to be deeply original and invariably provoke debate; *Breaking the Waves* (1996) is the latest. Here he is posing nonchalantly for the photographer. He fills out the whole picture-frame, radiating self-confidence, looking as if he is viewing with arrogant anticipation his future world audience.

T.T.

1983 (1991)
Gelatine silver print
39.4 x 32.9 cm
Frederiksborg
Museum

Lars von Trier, film director

85 | Morten Krogvold born 1950
Piet Hein 1905–1996

Like an old Chinese mandarin, Piet Hein – the writer, philosopher, inventor and academic – is sitting with crossed arms and protruding stomach. The pose is self-conscious and yet nonchalant. A penetrating gaze reveals his intellectual power.

Morten Krogvold has placed Hein centrally against a neutral background. The darkness around his figure is dissipated towards the four corners and gives the otherwise substantial body an almost floating dimension.

Krogvold, who was born in Norway, works as an international portrait photographer. He makes no secret of the pride he takes in having studied under the Canadian Yosuf Karsh.

T.T.

1993
Gelatine silver print
56.8 x 46.4 cm
Frederiksborg
Museum

Piet Hein, writer, inventor and philosopher

86 | Piotr Topperzer born 1948
Alev Siesbye born 1938

Alev Siesbye, née Ebüzzia, is one of Denmark's leading ceramic artists. She was trained at the Turkish Academy of Art in Istanbul from 1956 to 1958, and at the same time studied under the Turkish potter Füreya. In 1969 she opened her own atelier in Copenhagen, but she now lives some of the time in Paris. She has created a style which is completely her own, with its roots in the Turkish tradition and yet also inspired by Danish craft design from the post-war period.

The portrait of Alev Siesbye was taken in her own atelier. In the background shelves and a potter's wheel with a ceramic bowl can be seen. The dark wreath of hair around her face, resting on the beautiful strong hand, and the heavy though simple jewellery, join with the steady gaze to impart a strikingly authentic impression.

T.T.

1993
Gelatine silver print
50.3 x 60.6 cm
Frederiksborg
Museum

Alev Siesbye, ceramic artist

87 | Piotr Topperzer born 1948
Maurice (Martin) Drouzy born 1923

The French-born Catholic priest Martin Drouzy is a lecturer in Film Studies at the University of Copenhagen. He has written several books on the film-maker Carl Theodor Dreyer (1889–1968). The religious and existentialist themes in Dreyer's films have found an interpreter of unusual skill in Drouzy. The portrait, like cat. nos. 86 and 88, forms part of Topperzer's portrait series *I Danmark er jeg* (In Denmark I am). The title plays on the first line of a song written by Hans Christian Andersen: 'In Denmark I Was Born, there do I belong'. The title of the portrait-series leaves out the word 'born', significantly, because the one common denominator linking these 37 people photographed by Topperzer is that they were not born in Denmark. They are immigrants who have settled permanently in Denmark and who have each achieved distinction in his or her own field. The series belongs to the Frederiksborg Museum's National Portrait collection.

T.T.

1993
Gelatine silver print
50.3 x 60.6 cm
Frederiksborg
Museum

Maurice Drouzy, priest and film-historian

88 | Piotr Topperzer born 1948
Henrik, Prince of Denmark born 1934

This informal portrait photograph of the Prince Consort was taken in 1993 in the royal wine-cellar in Fredensborg Palace. After a formal photographic session in one of the main rooms of the palace the Prince suggested to the photographer that they go down to the wine-cellar to taste the wine and take photographs. With his characteristic irony the Prince often describes himself as 'prince and wine-grower'. On the estate of his château in his native Cahors in France he produces his own wine. The portrait belongs to the series 'In Denmark am I'. In 1969 the Prince married the eldest daughter of Frederik IX, Princess Margrethe, who succeeded her father on the throne of Denmark in 1972.

The photographer Piotr Topperzer, born in Poland, is himself a first generation immigrant to Denmark. He earns his living as a commercial photographer, but also finds time for the very personal and engaged work of which this series is an example.

T.T.

1993
Gelatine silver print
50.3 x 60,6 cm
Frederiksborg
Museum

His Royal Highness Prince Henrik of Denmark, Prince Consort

89 | Ole Haupt born 1944
Victor Borge (Børge Rosenbaum) born 1909

In the summer of 1996 the pianist Victor Borge visited his native
country, Denmark, for his annual performance in Tivoli. On that
occasion Ole Haupt photographed him sitting at an imaginary piano,
lifting his hands as though he was about to play. He is at the same time
looking straight at the eyes of the audience. He is ready. The 87-
year-old pianist and composer is an entertainer of world class. Strict
discipline emanates from his whole body, but the disconcertingly
ambiguous expression also commands attention: he wears the look of
the serious clown.

1996
Gelatine silver print
50.5 x 50.5 cm
Frederiksborg
Museum

Ole Haupt is himself both a musician and a photographer. He has
specialized in portraits of actors and musicians, but is also a traditional reporting photographer. His success in capturing the true
personality of the world-famous entertainer was due to the inalienable
sense of humour of both parties. Ole Haupt introduced himself not as
a portrait photographer but as a dissatisfied member of the audience,
coming to make a complaint. The half-hour sitting which he had
originally been allowed was expanded to more than two hours of
intense photographic work.

T.T.

Victor Borge, pianist

90 | Joyce Tenneson born 1945
Synnøve Søe born 1962

In 1990 the American artist Joyce Tenneson was invited to Denmark and to the American Embassy in Copenhagen to create her own series of images about Danes. She brought with her a 50 x 60 Polaroid Studio. She is one of the few people who have worked with this large-scale instant camera in recent years.

Synnøve Søe was part of the Copenhagen punk scene in the 1980s. She was known for her white cosmetic face-mask, which she wore night and day in mourning for her parents (who were not dead). As the child of parents who were among the creators of the social, moral and cultural upheavals of the 1960s, she has told her own side of the story, seen from a child's point of view, in novels based on autobiographical material.

In Tenneson's portrait she is wearing her white mask and a back-to-front corset. Her defiant posture is captured by the photographer as 'a closed field of forces'.

T.T.

1990
Polaroid '50 x 60
Studio'
80 x 56 cm
Frederiksborg
Museum

Synnøve Søe, writer

91

Joyce Tenneson born 1945
Agner Ahm born 1936

As a photographer and artist Joyce Tenneson has developed a unique style, particularly when she works with the large 50 x 60 Studio Camera, which weighs 90 kg. The photographic technique she used for the series entitled 'Great Danes' requires intense concentration. One can compare the polaroid photographs with the early portrait photographs from the last century, the daguerreotypes of the 1840's . In both cases the pictures are direct positives and the size is determined by the camera format.

Agner Ahm was previously chief-editor of the daily newspaper *Politiken,* one of Denmark's leading newspapers. In Joyce Tenneson's portrait his distinctive profile is reminiscent of the portraits of the Early Italian Renaissance.

T.T.

1990
Polaroid '50 x 60
Studio'
80 x 56 cm
Frederiksborg
Museum

Agner Ahm, chief-editor

92 | Jørgen Johansson born 1960
Sten Jørgensen born 1959

The lead singer from the group *Sort Sol* (Black Sun), Sten Jørgensen, is the subject of one of a series of four portraits in which each member of the now classic Danish rock group was photographed individually, on purpose, and not as a group. Their specific personalities become clearly apparent.

The photographer followed the group in order to film live during a concert. It struck him forcefully that these four people, in spite of their differences, made up the group *Sort Sol,* and that it had existed for more than ten years.

Jørgen Johansson uses an old large-format camera and makes deliberate use of a slow and intricate technique. He works mostly as a cameraman, but otherwise his photography is exclusively concerned with the human face, the portrait.

T.T.

1996
Gelatine silver print
47.5 x 40 cm
Frederiksborg
Museum

Sten Jørgensen, composer and singer

93 | Torben Eskerod born 1960
Kirsten Delholm born 1945

In 1991, after having studied architecture and engineering science, Torben Eskerod threw himself into portrait-photography. He is self-taught and is one of the few young photographers who works exclusively with portraits. Together with one of his more experienced colleagues he devised a challenging project involving the production by both photographers of portraits of one and the same subject, and the results were displayed in an exhibition entitled 'Portrait ^{2}', in 1995, in which this portrait of Kirsten Delholm was one of the exhibits.

Kirsten Delholm is a performance artist and the founder of the group *Hotel Pro Forma;* since the 1980s she has developed her own transcultural art-form, in which mime, movement, music and light are fused into performance. Eskerod's close-up portrait shows the passionately involved artist deeply engaged in creative work. The photographer has conveyed his impression of the subject's charisma in a very direct way, without attempting to flatter. Hand and face are given equal weight as elements in the picture. Written on the hand is the name of Delholm's husband, which was included at her explicit request.

T.T.

1995
Gelatine silver print
60.4 x 50.3 cm
Frederiksborg
Museum

Kirsten Delholm, performance artist

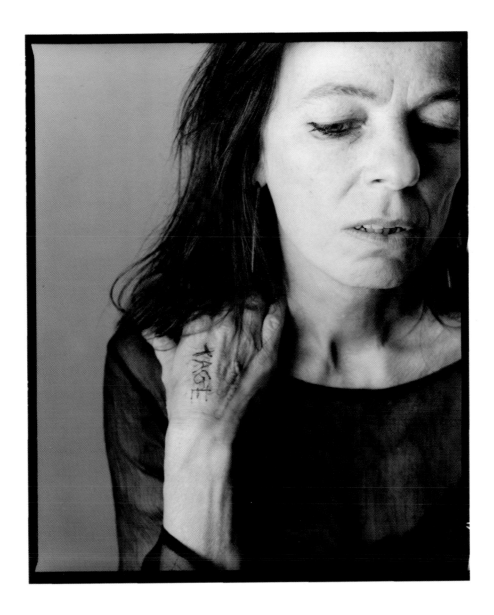

94 | Henrik Saxgren born 1953
Peter Schmeichel born 1963

Peter Schmeichel is the goal-keeper of the Danish football team – the team which won the European Championship in 1992. In the same year he was named the best goal-keeper in the world. He currently plays for Manchester United.

 The portrait of Schmeichel forms part of a series of photographic portraits of prominent Danes born after 1945 which was commissioned by the Frederiksborg Museum. This signalled the introduction of the modern 'story-telling' portrait into the collection.

 Henrik Saxgren is a leading documentary photographer who had not previously worked in the portrait genre before this commission. With his portrait of Schmeichel he wanted to describe not only the football-star but also his fans. The portrait was taken in a mine outside Manchester, and the men surrounding the tall blond Dane are miners. The portrait of the sports-star thus takes on an unexpected social dimension, and the viewer is confronted with the question of whether aesthetic effects can influence social debate.

T.T.

1993
Gelatine silver print
50.2 x 60.7 cm
Frederiksborg
Museum

Peter Schmeichel, football player

95 | Henrik Saxgren born 1953
Peter Høeg born 1957

"The first time I met Henrik Saxgren was on a bitingly cold autumn day in 1993. At first glance I suspected that he was a fanatic. An hour later I was certain of it." It is with these words that Peter Høeg introduces Henrik Saxgren's photographs in the photographer's recent book *POV*; Høeg thus simultaneously gives us indications about the two persons involved, one on one side of the camera and one on the other. The place where the photography was carried out was a deserted beach south-east of Copenhagen. The time: autumn. The session lasted half a day.

Peter Høeg was photographed immediately after he had published the book *Miss Smilla's Feeling for Snow*. The portrait reveals a young author in all his vulnerability. The strength of his gaze and the simplicity of the composition make this an extraordinarily striking portrait.

T.T.

1993
Gelatine silver print
45.5 x 60.4 cm
Frederiksborg
Museum

Peter Høeg, writer

96 Henrik Saxgren <small>born 1953</small>
Eva Fjellerup <small>born 1962</small>

This portrait, like cat. no. 94, is part of the series of prominent Danes born after 1945. The photographer took his own portable studio with him for the photographic sessions. Here, in the public swimming baths, the backcloth which is used consistently in the portraits is clearly in evidence. It is a tarpaulin. By using it as the background for all the portraits the photographer has created a form of coherence in the process of portrayal of the many different personalities involved. He has captured the moment where the swimmer comes darting out of the pool, and thereby created a tension between the frozen movement and the physical power radiating from the four-times-over world champion in pentathlon.

T.T.

1993
Gelatine silver print
60.8 x 50.5 cm
Frederiksborg
Museum

Eva Fjellerup, athlete

97

Rigmor Mydtskov born 1925
Frits Helmuth born 1931

Frits Helmuth, one of Denmark's leading male actors, can be seen reflected in a mirror-cabinet set up by Rigmor Mydtskov in 1996. With this arrangement the photographer has recreated an old photographic artifice which was very popular around the turn of the century, and she calls her series of mirror-cabinet portraits 'Company' (cf. cat. no 98). The fact that the subject is photographed from the back, in front of two mirrors placed at an angle of 72° and is thus seen five times over, means that he appears to be in company with others. Only after a moment's inspection does the viewer understand that it is one and the same person.

The actor Frits Helmuth, whose face is most often seen in the guise of a character, is seen here bare-faced. One can nevertheless feel a hint, from the multiple faces, of the actor's ability to create many characters. The profile on the right in particular brings to mind for all Danes the subject's famous father, the popular singer and revue actor Osvald Helmuth (1894–1966).

T.T.

1996
Gelatine silver print, RC-coated
66.4 x 125.8 cm
Frederiksborg Museum

Frits Helmuth, actor

98

Rigmor Mydtskov born 1925
Rose Gad born 1968

The ballerina's back and fine posture are particularly expressive in this photograph, which belongs to the portrait series 'Company' (cf. cat. no. 97), because of the placing of the camera behind the subject. In contrast to the other portraits in the series this contains an element of movement, and the riddle of the mirrors seems even more puzzling on account of this.

Among the most important roles in the repertoire of the Danish Royal Ballet are *Giselle,* which Rose Gad danced for the first time in 1990, and the main role in *La Sylphide,* created in 1836 by August Bournonville, the Danish choreographer of Romantic ballet.

The mirror pictures of Rose Gad are a tribute to the Danish Royal Ballet, which has maintained the position of Bournonville as a trump card. No other company in the world has such a large repertoire from the Romantic period.

Rigmor Mydtskov has functioned as photographer for the Danish Royal Ballet for more than 40 years.

T.T.

1996
Gelatine silver
print, RC-coated
66.4 x 125.8 cm
Frederiksborg
Museum

Rose Gad, solo dancer, Danish Royal Ballet

99 | Per Morten Abrahamsen born 1957
Bjarne Riis born 1965

In July 1996 the cyclist Bjarne Riis won the Tour de France, the world's most difficult and most prestigious cycle race.

Bjarne Riis has had a long career as a sportsman, but this historic event was his crowning achievement. In the course of his career he has become known as 'the eagle from Herning' (his birth-place); looking at the photograph one has to wonder whether the eagle is taking off, or has landed.

Per Morten Abrahamsen's staged portrait of this national hero artfully intertwines the nickname and the sports myth. Nowadays there is a process by which sports heroes become national, publicly owned property, but with strong national and religious undertones. The image has been created in the media spotlights, but also of course in the cyclist's actual conquest of the mountain and of himself. Without his bicycle, and yet still in motion, like a space hero created by the electronic media, Riis makes his appearance: a revelation. Behind him is the conspicuous expanse of horizon and the arch of a metallic blue sky.

T.T.

1996
Colour photograph
from colour
negative (Kodak)
90 x 70 cm
Frederiksborg
Museum

Bjarne Riis, racing cyclist

Index of Artists

Index of Sitters